YOUR
BEAUTIFUL
Destiny

A HEALING JOURNEY THROUGH
CHILDHOOD SEXUAL ABUSE

CHRISTINA DUKE

Dorothy Ann Publishing
www.DorothyAnnPublishing.com
cduke@dorothyannpublishing.com

ISBN: Paperback 979-8-9989070-0-5
ISBN: ebook 979-8-9989070-1-2

Library of Congress Control Number: 2025909713

This book is a memoir. It reflects the author's present recollections of experiences over time. Some names and identifying details have been changed to protect the privacy of individuals.

Printed in the United States of America
First Edition: 2025

Table of Contents

Disclaimer

This book is a personal memoir based on my experiences. Some names, identifying details, locations, and timelines have been altered. Although I changed some details to maintain confidentiality, the emotions, struggles, and healing journey accurately reflect my lived experience.

This book contains discussions of childhood trauma, abuse and sensitive topics that may be distressing or triggering for some readers. If you have experienced similar trauma, please read with care and ensure you have the support you need. You are not alone, and help is available.

This book's content is not a substitute for professional therapy, counseling, or medical advice. If you or someone you know is struggling, please reach out to a trusted professional or support resource. Healing is possible, and support is within reach.

Foreword

As an ordained Elder in the Free Methodist Church and a Licensed Clinical Mental Health Counselor, I've spent years walking beside individuals as they navigate the complex terrain of trauma and healing. Few stories have impacted me as deeply as Christina Duke's.

Over the past year, I've had the privilege of working with Christina in a professional capacity and have witnessed firsthand the raw courage, deep faith, and unwavering determination that define her journey. *Your Beautiful Destiny* is not simply a memoir; it is a sacred offering. It is the unflinching, heartfelt testimony of a woman who refused to let childhood sexual trauma define the rest of her life.

In these pages, Christina invites us into some of her most vulnerable moments, not to shock or sensationalize, but to illuminate a path forward. She does not minimize the pain. She does not rush past the devastation. Instead, she bravely lays bare the lasting impact of abuse and the painstaking work it takes to heal from it. Her story is anchored in honesty, guided by faith, and rooted in the belief that wholeness is not only possible, it is promised.

What sets this memoir apart is the way Christina invites God into every chapter of her healing. She recognizes that while trauma may fracture the soul, restoration can be found through grace, truth, and the loving presence of those who choose to walk alongside us. As someone who was honored to serve as one of those guides during her journey, I have seen God's hand move powerfully through Christina's life. Her transformation is both a testimony and a roadmap.

This book is not just for survivors, though they will undoubtedly find comfort, validation, and hope here. It is also for loved ones, counselors, pastors, and anyone seeking to understand the depth of trauma and the strength it takes to rise from it. Christina's story reminds us that while trauma may mark a beginning, it does not define the end.

If you or someone you love has experienced childhood sexual abuse, may this book be a light in the darkness. May it remind you that healing is possible. That peace is attainable. And that your beautiful destiny is still ahead of you.

William R. Powell
Licensed Clinical Mental Health Counselor
Ordained Elder, Free Methodist Church

Dedication

Dedicated to my grandmother, Marilyn Elaine Santoro. Your boundless love and strength were my guiding light during life's most challenging times. You taught me resilience and reminded me to stand strong, no matter the storms. Your strength, safety, and courage have been a blessing to me. Every word and step of my journey reflects the perseverance you fostered in me. I'm forever grateful for your wisdom and warmth.

To the reader: Thank you for your courage in choosing this book and for your self-reflection. I dedicate this to all who have faced adversity and survived, bearing their marks with pride or in continued recovery. Hopefully, my story will inspire your own healing journey, showing that it's worthwhile despite its flaws and continuous process. Remember that you are stronger than you believe, and you are never walking this path by yourself. May you discover serenity, resilience, and the knowledge that your beautiful destiny awaits.

Preface

The undertaking of writing *Your Beautiful Destiny* was more profound than I initially expected. Writing encompassed more than mere words; every page presented unexpected challenges, compelling me to unearth buried memories and face realities I wasn't sure I could handle. Despite the pain and vulnerability, I discovered my purpose.

This memoir is for my younger self and anyone who has felt unheard, invisible, or inadequate. If you're struggling with trauma and despair, know that recovery is possible, healing is achievable, and your story matters.

This is an unfiltered story of a life shaped by abuse, neglect, and the constant yearning for love and connection. It is about learning to get back up and rise, even when the weight of the world feels unbearable. Discovering hope amidst despair teaches us that healing is a nonlinear, messy, painful, yet profoundly transformative journey.

The strength found in shared experiences, knowing others have faced similar struggles, led me to share my story. If my story helps even one person feel less isolated and gives them a little hope, then all the anguish of writing it will have been worthwhile.

Your Beautiful Destiny is not merely my personal narrative; rather, it serves as an invitation, a call to action, emphasizing that confronting the painful memories of the past is fundamentally essential for wholeheartedly embracing a hopeful future. It's a reminder that healing is not about erasing what happened but about reclaiming your narrative and choosing to live boldly, despite it all.

For those who've felt broken or lost, please know you are not alone. The strength you've shown is clear in your survival and your story. Though you can't see it yet, beauty awaits you, even after the storm has passed. I want to uplift you and show you that you have the potential to overcome challenges.

I'm grateful for the opportunity to share my journey with you. May these pages inspire courage, hope, and the confidence that you are worthy of joy, healing, and a beautiful destiny.

—Christina Duke

Letter To My Younger Self

Dear Christina,

I know you feel alone. I know you feel like the world is pressing down on you while trapping you in silence and fear. As a warrior, you stand tangled in confusion, struggling with secrets others wrongly burdened you with. You've suffered things no child should, and I wish I could go back in time, hold you close, and whisper the words you've always longed to hear. You deserved love, safety, and laughter. Instead, you received pain.

It's true; those who should have protected you let you down. You think you're damaged, unworthy, and stained by the weight of others' sins, but none of this is true. You are pure, strong, and beautiful in ways you don't yet understand. Despite the cracks and imbalance in your world, you are the most courageous person I know. Strength lies in your tears, every breath you held, and each step forward when you want to hide.

Little warrior, one day, light will shine through the darkness. I wish you could see her now, your future self, standing tall, heart softened but unbreakable. You'll spend years searching for love in all the wrong places, seeking validation from people who don't deserve your heart. People will exploit your vulnerability. Healing will be difficult, but eventually you'll realize you're complete on your own.

Days will come when anger consumes you like a fire. You'll want to scream, fight, or disappear, and there will be times you'll feel like a stranger in your own skin, and that's okay. Reclaiming yourself will be a long journey and worth every step. Along the way, you will discover you are more than your scars, more than the names they called you, and more than the past that tried so hard to keep you down. You'll forgive, not because they deserve it, but because you deserve peace.

Motherhood will bring immense love but also challenges. Your pain will transform you and you will become overprotective to safeguard your children from the darkness that plagued your life.

Through trial and error, you will learn that the best protection you can give your children is a mother who is healing, a mother who is breaking cycles, a mother who believes in her own worth. You'll find strength to do right, even when decisions are hard. Know that your children will feel that love, no matter how much you sometimes doubt yourself.

Knowing your strength and determination fills me with pride. From broken pieces, your resiliency will create a life worth living. You will carve out meaning from pain and find something beautiful: you will find **yourself.**

Precious one, carry this forward with you: you are enough. You deserve love, happiness, and a life free from fear. Don't let what others did to you define you. Your presence makes the world brighter and stronger. Hold on even in those moments when you feel like giving up. Your best is yet to come.

Sending you all my love,
The Woman You Will Become

YOUR BEAUTIFUL
Destiny

If she could put the hollow ache that haunts her into words, she would tell him,
"I miss the father you never were."
John Mark Green

PART 1

FATHERLESS DAUGHTER

CHAPTER 1

THE MASK OF NORMALCY

WHEN I WAS NOT attending school or visiting our extended family with Mama, I lived in solitude, mostly outdoors, rain or shine, as far away from home as I could get. I filled my days climbing trees, chasing the majestic peacocks on our property, or playing recklessly near the creek at our one-story red brick home in Loomis, California. As a child of the 80s, I thrived on juicy yellow pears from our backyard trees and stayed hydrated with hose water. I quickly learned to let the hose run to flush out the scalding water that had collected inside and to avoid unexpected encounters with spiders, crickets, or slugs flying into my mouth as I turned it on. Some mistakes you only make once. Like the revolting taste of a slimy slug mixed with boiling hose water.

During one especially memorable weekend, my mother and I journeyed to the home of her elder sister, my Aunt Patricia, a place that always seemed vibrant with the sounds of laughter and the enticing fragrance of delicious food simmering on the stove. My cousins Jackson and Maryann were running wild, joined by neighborhood children, transforming the cul-de-sac into a buzzing hive of energy. I spent most of the day watching them and their friends ride their bikes, weaving through the streets like a pack of professional bike racers. They popped wheelies, raced each other back and forth, and laughed as they pedaled away with effortless speed. I sat on the curb, watching, my little legs bouncing in frustration. I wanted in. There was just one problem: At six years old, I was still wobbling around on a bike that had training wheels attached, while my cousins zoomed back and forth like they were training for the BMX Olympics. I needed to learn, and I needed to learn now.

Determined, I begged to borrow a bike. My cousin Jackson, however, was not feeling generous. Honestly, I couldn't blame him. The last time I visited, I took his shiny new Huffy mountain bike for an unauthorized joyride. Despite the fact that my feet could barely reach the pedals on his enormous bicycle, I was certain that I could figure out how to ride it independently. I pedaled with reckless determination, until, of course, I lost control, veered off the sidewalk, and crashed directly into a tree. The aftermath was a bent frame, scratched-up paint, a bike that looked like it had gone through a battlefield, and one very pissed-off Jackson. He hadn't forgiven me for that tragic bike homicide, and now, here I was asking for another chance.

"Yeah, not happening." Jackson snarled as he towered over me, clutching his bike like it was his firstborn child, shooting me a glare that screamed, *Not today, Satan, no way!*

"Last time you almost totaled my bike!" he huffed, rolling his eyes as he straddled the seat, ready to ride off.

"But I learned!" I protested, lying through my teeth, and clasping my hands in dramatic desperation. "I swear I won't crash this time!"

He wasn't buying it.

"Never going to happen. I like my bike in one piece," he shot back before pedaling away, leaving me standing there, defeated.

With my arms folded, I watched enviously as they rode around me. My body heated with frustration. I wanted to be part of the fun and ride, too. That day, I made a vow to myself: I would learn to ride a bike. I didn't know when; I didn't know how, but one day, I'd be flying down the street just like them, without training wheels, without crashing, and without having to beg. For now, I was stuck on the curb, dreaming of the day I'd get my revenge on gravity and Jackson.

From that day on, all I wanted was a bike of my own. I begged my parents relentlessly, and finally Daddy helped me assemble one using discarded bike parts salvaged from neighborhood trash and junk yards. Together, we built a bike. It was mostly purple with a frame covered in nicks and dings, revealing raw metal. While others might have seen it as a mishmash or embarrassment, to me, it was a gift from the gods. I beamed with pride over my glorious purple and silver bike, despite its lack of brakes or gears. My purple prize was all I needed; now, I just had to learn to ride it.

I spent many afternoons practicing on my bike, starting at the top of the hill in our backyard. I'd balance myself and let gravity pull me downhill at full speed. My rides usually ended when I ran out of momentum as the terrain evened out, or, on some occasions when I was really going, I would crash into the neighbors' chain-link fence to stop. Hours of trial and error, driven by my unwavering determination, led to scraped knees and epic crashes, but also to the exhilarating thrill of mastering a new skill.

Sometimes, Daddy would attempt to teach me by holding the seat as I tried to balance and coordinate my hands and feet to pedal the bike. I desperately needed help, but the thought of him giving it to me filled me with dread. While sitting still on the bike, concentrating on maintaining my balance, I sensed a pull on my shirt. With his other hand, he slipped his sweaty hand down my shorts, grabbing my buttocks, causing me to momentarily lose focus. I would swiftly steady myself, but I understood the unsettling implications of his actions. I could sense that if I didn't escape, things would escalate, and he would insist I join him in the garage again. All I wanted was to ride my bike. I purposely would lose my balance, tumble off dramatically, and pretend to hurt my arm. Insisting I needed comfort from Mama, I hurried inside before he could convince me otherwise. Mama's presence was a shield against Daddy's touch. I sought refuge in her embrace, hoping for protection.

Making my way through the back door, I called out loudly to catch her attention so she could rescue me from Daddy's hidden play time. She was nowhere in sight. As I ventured into the front yard, I noticed the family car was missing. Daddy caught up with me and demanded that I retrieve the bike I had left in the backyard and put it away in the garage. My puzzlement stemmed from having just gotten the bike and always leaving it where I'd last ridden it. I thought, why did I need to put it in the garage this time? I acted like I did not hear him and headed to the living room to sit down and watch cartoons, sensing that this was his way of luring me into the garage so he could continue what he had begun.

Next came the forceful thump to the back of my head. My little body jerked forward from the impact, a dull pain radiating through my skull. I barely had time to register the sting before Daddy's deep, stern voice cut through the thick evening air.

"Pick up that damn bike and put it in the garage!"

His voice wasn't just angry, it was that dangerous mad, the kind that made my gut tangle in knots. I had triggered his rage again. By now, I had learned the rhythm of his anger. When Daddy was upset, it meant one thing: he was going to hit me, throw me, and hurt me. In those moments, I at least knew his hands wouldn't wander to places they shouldn't. When he was angry, his focus was on punishment, not on the other things he did when the house was quiet, when no one else was around to witness it.

That thought alone made the sharp pain in my scalp easier to bear. I clenched my teeth, swallowing the instinct to cry.

"I'll give you something to cry about." His favorite threat.

The words never made sense to my kindergarten brain. Wasn't I already crying? What more did he want? But I had learned the hard way that any sign of weakness, any tears, whimpers, or flinches, would only make things worse. So, I did what I always did. I locked it all inside the best I could and obeyed. I scrambled toward my bicycle, gripping the handlebars with shaky hands. My fingers fumbled as I hurriedly dragged it toward the garage, my tiny arms struggling against its weight. In my rush, I didn't bother setting it down carefully. I threw it inside, the metal frame clattering loudly against the concrete floor. I braced myself, half-expecting him to lash out again for the noise, but before he could react, I heard it. The sound of tires crunching against gravel. My heart leaped. I knew that sound like I knew the rhythm of my breathing, the unmistakable hum of my mother's car pulling into the driveway. Relief flooded so fast it made me lightheaded. For that moment, I knew I was safe.

As a young child, I was too young to fully grasp the weight of what was happening, yet old enough to feel its impact. My world was a place of contradictions, where love and fear existed simultaneously, and those supposed to protect me hurt me. My innocence clashed with my reality, creating an unstable mix of fear, confusion, and survival instincts. So, I did what any child would do. I sought safety in the few places I could find it.

Looking back, I realize now that my childhood adventures were more than just play. They were acts of survival, minor rebellions against the turbulence that threatened to consume me. Every time I escaped outside, I ran toward something greater than myself, a world untouched by pain, a space where I could breathe, move, and exist without fear. Nature became my refuge. Open fields, sturdy trees, and the endless sky above offered neither judgment, heavy hands, nor whispered threats. The wind didn't scold me, the dirt beneath my bare feet didn't bruise, and the sun never looked at me with anger. The outdoors was the only place I could be free, even if only for a little while.

I didn't know it then, but those moments were laying the groundwork for the person I would become. My initial experiences with independence involved exceeding permitted boundaries on lengthy bike rides. The hours spent wandering through neighborhoods, exploring, imagining. My first taste of freedom was the quiet moments sitting under trees, staring at the sky, and wondering about the future. They were the earliest sparks of resilience, the foundation of a fire that would one day burn bright.

Despite the challenges, the confusion, and the fear, I learned how to carve out pockets of peace in a life that often felt like a storm. That determination, that refusal to surrender to my circumstances, would become the driving force behind everything I would achieve later in life.

CHAPTER 2

SHATTERED BEGINNINGS

ONE EVENING MAMA SURPRISED me with a soft, new Care Bears nightgown that draped elegantly below my knees. Being taller than most kids my age meant my nightwear usually hovered awkwardly above the wrinkly part of my knees, unlike the little girl pictured on the packaging, whose nightgown flowed gracefully down to tickle her ankles. But none of that mattered to me: this wasn't another hand-me-down from my aunt, or something scavenged from donation boxes by the goodwill truck late at night. This was brand new, still in its original packaging, a Care Bears nightgown from Kmart, just for me! Excitedly, I soaked in the warm bubble bath Mama had prepared after dinner, eager to slip into my new nightgown and head straight to bed. In my mind, I embodied Bedtime Bear, though my pajamas featured Cheer Bear. Despite the mismatch, I felt special, cherished, and ready to drift off into a peaceful sleep.

There's an undeniable joy in slipping into new pajamas, even if you're settling into the comfort of familiar old sheets. As I christened my bed, rolling around to find the perfect spot, my battalion of stuffed animals stood guard. Strategically placed alongside me, they filled the gap where the bed met the wall, warding off any lurking monsters and keeping me safe from the dark abyss below. After Mama tucked me in, she'd utter her familiar bedtime sayings.

"Snug as a bug in a rug," followed by the less comforting, "Don't let the bedbugs bite," as she wrapped me in a burrito in my favorite blanket.

The warmth of her embrace and the security of being tucked in were the best feelings, but I never quite warmed up to those analogies. The idea of bed bugs, even metaphorical ones, nestled with me, always making me shudder. Many nights I would lie there analyzing the bugs, their location, size, and my defense strategy for the inevitable moment when they would strike.

Who even came up with that phrase? There are generations of parents unknowingly terrifying children.

Tonight, however, I felt different. For once, I pushed aside my usual mental anguish and worries. I don't remember when, but I must have drifted off peacefully, wrapped in warmth and the comfort of my cozy bed. All I knew was that darkness consumed me when I was abruptly awakened by the sensation of cold, rough hands pulling back my covers. Daddy's voice, usually warm and reassuring, now stern and hushed, instructed me to stay quiet and not wake Mama. I obeyed, instinctively wrapping my arms around his neck and my legs around his waist, mimicking the way parents carry their sleeping children. Together, we tiptoed through the house. The only light was a faint glow seeping through heavy curtains, casting a dim outline of the furniture and creating shadows that danced across the walls. As we passed through the living room and kitchen, the faint light revealed the midnight sky adorned with bright stars. It wasn't until we stepped outside the front door that I fully woke up. The crisp night air hit me like a wave, sending goose bumps racing across my skin. The breeze carried a sharpness that cut through my new nightgown, much like the thorns in Grandma Denise's rose garden. Grandma always cautioned me to admire the roses with my eyes, not my hands. But I couldn't resist the temptation to touch the soft, waxy petals. When no one was looking, I would sneak a rose, inevitably pricking my stubborn fingers on the thorns.

My eyes slowly adjusted to the darkness as we crept behind the hefty front yard boulder, about the size of a dishwasher that sat just out of view from the living room window. It was my favorite rock to climb during the day, often needing a boost to reach its peak when I enacted my famous game of Imaginary Princess on the Mountain. But tonight was different. Were we playing that game now? The darkness cloaked everything, casting doubt on whether I could see my forest animals below. What about Ken, my Barbie doll prince, who always came to my rescue? Realization struck suddenly. We had forgotten my box of toys. How could we possibly play without them? Panic flickered through my mind, but Daddy's firm grip and secretive urgency pressed me to stay silent and follow his command.

I clung tightly to him for warmth as he bent down, carefully releasing my legs and then my arms before gently lowering me to the ground. The grass was cold and damp. I could feel the moisture on my thighs and my panties absorbed the fresh dew. In hindsight, I believe it was that eerie time when night yielded to the early morning hours. His familiar voice comforted me as he introduced an unfamiliar activity that did not feel good but also did not feel bad, just different and strange.

He had touched my bottom before, weirdly, but this time was different. All I yearned for was to return to the comfort of my warm, cozy bed. His hands helped themselves to places on my body that I could barely identify; all I understood was that when I felt the need to use the bathroom, it came from that area. Mama taught me the importance of keeping that part of my body clean, instructing me to wash it with the washcloth after I washed my face during bath time. Oh, and she always reminded me to use soap on the rag, I'd sometimes forget. Why was he so interested in my area? Why did we have to be outside in the cold for him to do whatever he was doing? Bewildered, I couldn't grasp what was happening.

Then, the pain hit me like a lightning bolt. A sharp, burning sensation shot through my area like a hot knife, and I yelped in pain, momentarily forgetting that I was supposed to be quiet not to wake Mama. The pain was unlike any I had experienced in my six short years of life thus far. It was unbearable. It brought tears to my eyes, and I struggled to keep them hidden. Daddy didn't tolerate my crying; it only angered him further. His voice, once soothing, turned harsh and frightening. He leaned so close I could feel his breath in my ear.

"Shut the fuck up!" He grabbed my arm firmly with his other hand, still hurting my area. I felt cold, wet, and utterly uncomfortable with this experience, though I couldn't quite grasp what was happening. All I knew was that I wanted it to end. I wanted to return to the warmth of the house. I expressed my distress as clearly as any upset kindergartener could. It must have worked because his hands became soft and fled my area, relieving the pressure and pain of this uncomfortable new experience. He held my freezing, damp body close as he carried me back to my now chilled bed.

My next memory was Mama gently waking me up for school. Despite my tired and grouchy demeanor, Mama didn't seem alarmed. Perhaps my behavior wasn't out of the ordinary for early mornings. However, my semi-routine of having an accident in my panties at night prompted Daddy to spank me. I dreaded having accidents at night, knowing what would follow. Mama, in her sweet yet firm way, reminded me again that I should wake up to use the bathroom and not wet my panties.

Don't cry, hide the tears, I coached myself, but this time, the sting of Daddy's hand on my backside was harder than usual. I couldn't help but cry, the memory of being on the damp grass flooding back.

"But I didn't have an accident. The grass was—"

"You better shut up. That is our secret. If you say anything, you will be in big trouble," Daddy whispered.

I imagine most children recall their childhood homes with distinct features, such as the brick house adorned with a tire swing and a bright red door, or the gray house nestled in a cul-de-sac surrounded by lush fruit trees. That's cute! I remember the twisted perversions and beatings and sexual abuse in my California childhood homes. Our home in Loomis was the house where Daddy first touched me. In Carmichael, our home bore the painful memory of Daddy's steel-toed boot kicking me in the shin. The brief stay with in-laws in Sacramento was where Daddy would lead me to the basement storage area, permeated with the scent of mold and overrun with black widow spiders. Despite the dangerous arachnids, their venom was the least of my worries. I welcomed their venomous bite over his poisonous touch. In Elk Grove, our last home as the Blackwell family, memories resonated with a blend of warmth and tension. Ultimately, Elk Grove serves as an emotional landmark in my history, where the fragile nature of family bonds became painfully clear as they shattered into pieces. It marked the end of my journey as Daddy's daughter and the beginning of a new chapter in foster care.

CHAPTER 3

BENEATH THE SURFACE

THE NEXT MORNING, MY excitement to get to school overshadowed any lingering confusion about the previous night's mysterious excursion behind the boulder. Perhaps it was all just a weird dream. At school this week it was my turn to bask in the glory, wear the crown and embrace the title of Queen of the Week. Ms. Applegate, our petite kindergarten teacher, stood a mere five feet on a good day and had flowing black hair that cascaded down her back. She always wore a smile that could light up the room. Her hair often tickled my face as she leaned over our desks to assist with tasks, a small but endearing annoyance that we giggled about whenever she turned away.

After reciting the pledge of allegiance, Ms. Applegate called me to the front of the class.

"Christina, it's your turn to be Queen of the Week." Ms. Applegate motioned me to the front of the class.

I grasped my place on the royal stool, adjusting my crown with the poise of a princess. Wearing the crown of the week's monarch was a privilege every student cherished and coveted. It came with perks like leading the line, having first dibs on dodge ball, and occupying the coveted front desk, to name a few. Throughout morning circle time and art class, I constantly adjusted my crown and stole glances at my reflection in the windows and the sink mirror during repeated hand washing sessions. Students could wear their crown during class, but had to leave it inside during lunch and recess.

As recess approached, I carefully placed my crown on my desk and proudly took my place at the front of the line, relishing my newfound status. Brian Matthews, the class troublemaker who loved disrupting order, swiftly challenged my moment of triumph. He rudely cut in front of me, attempting to take my honorary position. Determined to uphold my earned status, I reminded him of his place and sidestepped him to reclaim mine. However, as I focused on the playground rules posted on the heavy green door, I felt a sudden shove from behind.

Turning around in shock, Brian spit on my purple corduroy overalls. Although they were a bit out of season for the beginning of summer, I cherished them dearly. Fueled by a mix of indignation and confusion over Brian's barbaric act, I squared my shoulders and retaliated with a forceful push. Brian's scrawny frame collided with a nearby desk, causing it to flip over as he crashed to the ground.

Silence fell over the class, broken only by my cry, "He spit on me, Ms. Applegate!"

I stormed off to the classroom sink, scrubbing Brian's spit from my precious overalls. Ms. Applegate helped Brian up, who had instantly transformed into a tearful victim. Her stern voice reprimanded me for my impulsive reaction as she filled out the familiar pink referral slip that would send me to Principal Harrington's office. Making my way down the well-trodden path to the main office, I mourned in that moment, as I knew the consequences of my actions would cause me losing my cherished queen status.

Waiting in the office, Mrs. Brown, the school secretary, glared at me with undisguised contempt. Her usual disdainful remarks felt insignificant compared to the impending punishment awaiting me at home. Daddy had been called to pick me up, and I dreaded the inevitable beating that waited. When Daddy arrived, Mrs. Brown's demeanor shifted from disdain to an almost gleeful alertness.

"She's over there," she announced to Daddy, her voice dripping with disapproval.

Ignoring the tension, Daddy greeted her politely before heading to Principal Harrington's office for their customary discussion.

Daddy's smile faded as he escorted me to Principal Harrington's office, steering me firmly into a chair outside the door. With a stern look, he warned me that consequences were coming.

"Good morning, Robert," Daddy greeted the principal with the familiarity of old friends.

"Curtis, always a pleasure. I wish we could meet under better circumstances. Unfortunately, the young man she assaulted was too upset to go back to class today and had to be picked up by his mother."

"I apologize for Christina's behavior. I assure you; we will address this matter promptly when we get home," Daddy replied with a militant sternness.

I listened anxiously as they talked, trying to catch their words over Mrs. Brown's obnoxiously loud phone call. Though Brian spit on me first and pushed me, the ping-pong ball sized lump on the back of his head along with other inflated injuries, plus my rap sheet of previous offenses, painted me as a repeat offender.

Daddy nodded silently for me to follow him. Grabbing my worn green backpack, a relic from our late-night scavenges at Goodwill, I avoided eye contact and climbed into his maroon Toyota pickup truck. As we drove, I stared fixedly at the floorboards; I counted every piece of trash and pebbles that rested peacefully on the floor. The air was thick and sweat rolled down my back profusely. A queasy sensation filled the pit of my stomach, followed by an urge to get to the toilet immediately. The unsettling bubbles inside grew more and more intense.

"I have to go to the bathroom," I muttered, still avoiding his gaze.

"The only place you're going is to your room for an attitude adjustment," Daddy responded grimly, a phrase that always preceded the harshest punishments.

Arriving home, I followed him silently to my room. Passing the kitchen counter, he seamlessly grabbed the black leather belt with the giant gold buckle without skipping a beat. Upon entering my room, I dropped my purple corduroy overalls, letting them fall to my ankles. His disappointment and anger were palpable as he delivered each blow with stern precision, teaching me a hard lesson about the consequences of losing self-control. As the belt stung against my skin, I retreated into my mental sanctuary, disconnecting from the pain and madness around me. With frequent practice, I had mastered the art of disassociation whenever I faced unbearable situations. Finally, with a last shove of irritation, Daddy released his grip on my arm, letting me crumble to the floor.

For what felt like an eternity, I lay there on the filthy beige carpet, replaying last night's confusing visit and today's series of unfortunate events. Each blow from Daddy's belt echoed in my mind, amplifying my sense of defeat and misunderstanding. The stark realization struck me that neither school nor home felt safe or comforting. The weight of isolation and vulnerability settled heavily upon me, a burden I carried silently as tears stung my eyes.

CHAPTER 4

SEEKING SOLACE

MOVING TO CARMICHAEL A couple years later marked a turning point. At Coyle Elementary, I felt the first gust of freedom, an escape from the quiet pain of home and the cruel corridors of my previous school. Coyle felt like stepping into a different world, one where I could almost forget what might await me at home. I spent my weekdays in a state of relative normalcy, thanks to six hours of classes and three hours of the after-school child-care program.

At the after-school program, I immersed myself in arts and crafts. I became a favorite of Mrs. Marshal, a senior volunteer at Coyle's growing after-school program, who took me under her wing. I did not see it then, but after working in the childcare field as an adult and eventually owning a childcare business after leaving the military, I realized Mrs. Marshall was the only one who knew how to handle me. She harnessed my overflowing buckets of energy and ability to focus when bored by teaching me how to sew, create pinatas and paint.

Finding something I was interested in tapped into my ability to hyper-focus on a task, hence preventing the mischief I would otherwise cause if left in a bored state. I now call it my ADHD superpower: The ability to focus intently on learning new tasks, hobbies and writing, things I can do for hours on end. With minimal guidance, I fixated on stitching fabric, making pillows, crafting pinatas, and painting until my heart was content. I was proud of the small blue pillow I made using leftover scraps of corduroy fabric. Every crooked stitch felt like a minor victory as I wove the needle through the unforgiving fabric. Mrs. Marshall's repeated reminders to use the thimble replayed in my mind upon every painful push of a tiny silver needle that left my thumb riddled with indents. I finished my precious pillow after sitting still longer than I ever had before during my visits to the after-school program.

Admiring my hard work, I smiled with joy. Others might have seen a lumpy, unevenly shaped rectangular mess. I saw a beautiful masterpiece adorned with a handful of perfectly placed hard plastic gems that would eventually scratch my face upon attempting to sleep on it that night. I was proud of my independent work and eager to share it. My excitement, ADHD, and lack of manners led me to dart through the cluttered classroom like a bull in a China shop, knocking over a student's cup filled with paintbrush water, immediately destroying her prized masterpiece. Because I was not a complete jerk, I apologized to the now distraught student and reluctantly helped clean up the mess I had caused.

After what seemed to take hours in the eyes of a child, I was back at full speed in motion on a mission to share my pillow with Mrs. Marshall, who was at the front desk. Without getting two full strides in, Mrs. Luray, the fifth grade teacher in charge of the after-school program, commanded me to stop running, instantly derailing me. My long legs walked a bit more cautiously to the front desk, where Mrs. Marshall and another student were engaged in a conversation.

I blurted, "I finished, Mrs. Marshall. I finished my pillow!"

Pausing her conversation with the student, she slowly looked up, and with an annoyed but gentle smile, she kindly instructed me to wait my turn as she finished her conversation. My fidgeting while impatiently waiting had a way of concluding other people's conversations.

Finally, it was my turn. I grew nervous as Mrs. Marshal took the pillow from my hand and meticulously examined every detail. Thoughts of doubt raced through my mind and the light of excitement I had so proudly carried just a moment ago dimmed. What if she doesn't like it? What if it's not that good?

"This is beautiful work, Christina," she said, her voice warm and reassuring. "You should be proud of yourself."

Her words hit me like a gentle wave, taking that inner light from once dim to a spotlight. My excitement to receive her approval left me uncertain of how to respond, so I just nodded, trying to hide the growing smile tugging at my lips. Her approval was just what I needed and desperately craved.

Another of Coyle's amazing heroes was my third-grade teacher, Mrs. Lawson. She had a calmness that drew me in and seemed to understand me in a way that few adults did. Her genuine acknowledgement and recognition filled me with indescribable joy. For a child who felt invisible at home, that attention was everything. Her patience wrapped around me like a warm blanket on those days when I felt fragile. Even when I acted out, and I did act out, she exemplified patience and grace in a way that would later inspire me when I ventured into motherhood. A skill I never quite mastered, but a quest I continue to navigate.

My particularly obnoxious habit of commanding attention when things didn't go my way, or when I felt like I was fading into the background, often consumed Mrs. Lawson's precious instruction time. My behavior wasn't the most subtle, but it was the only way I knew how to express myself and garner the attention I craved. One afternoon, I began experiencing an uncontrollable case of the hiccups in class. The exaggerated frog-like noise erupting from my throat quickly became an amusing distraction. As the students began to giggle and point, I felt a strange mixture of embarrassment and satisfaction. I hated being the center of negative attention, but some attention was better than none. Mrs. Lawson, with her usual calm yet firm voice, guided the class back to order and respectfully insisted I step outside until my hiccups were gone. To my surprise, the hiccups stopped within a matter of minutes of stepping outside of the classroom.

No matter how much I tried to fit in at school, I always felt like an outsider. Friends were a luxury I did not possess, and during the few times I made a friend, that friendship ran its course faster than an Olympic runner in the 100-meter dash. Being a loner was something I was getting quite used to.

Lining up for lunch one warm late spring afternoon seemed to offer a glimmer of hope, the possibility of an unexpected new friendship. I found myself in my routine spot at the back of the lunch line, standing behind Ashley Montgomery, one of the most popular girls in my grade, who usually found her place closer to the front with the rest of the popular kids. With a bright smile and shoulder-length, perfectly straight blonde hair gleaming under the fluorescent lights, she looked as though she brushed it 100 times a day. Her bright blue eyes had a touch of innocence, which she often used to her advantage. Her well-coordinated and expensive wardrobe (for a third grader) was far more desirable than my secondhand Goodwill clothes. Although she appeared snobbish, she had never been unkind to me. That year, I could count on one hand the number of times she spoke to me.

Her lunches were always amazing: little sandwiches, fruit cups, and those decadent chocolate cupcakes with thick icing. I don't know what made her do it, but that afternoon she offered me her cupcake. I felt shocked and grateful at the same time. My gratitude and hopes of hanging out with her and her friends on the playground quickly turned sour when I overheard her after lunch telling the other girls that she gave it to me because she felt sorry for me. My cheeks burned with humiliation. At that moment, something shifted in me. A frustrated anger and embarrassment bubbled up like something I had not experienced before.

The next day, I watched Ashley's every move, waiting for the brief opportunity when I could catch her alone. She ran beside the building at recess to retrieve the ball as she and her friends carelessly enjoyed their popular kids' only kickball game. Seizing the opportunity, I cornered Ashley when she was out of sight and told her that if she didn't bring me a cupcake every day, I would beat her up. Taking a page out of Daddy's book, I threatened her not to tell anyone or I would really hurt her. It was an impulsive threat, one that I wasn't even sure I could follow through on, but the power of saying it, of flipping the script and taking control for once, felt intoxicating. She complied. Every day, she brought me a cupcake, and every day, I felt a little more powerful, but also a little emptier.

That empty feeling grew worse when my beloved hero, Mrs. Lawson, found out after only a few days into my devilish scheme. Her disappointment in my behavior was far more of a punishment than what I would receive from the principal and, eventually, from Daddy. I lost my privilege to go on the highly anticipated end-of-year trip to Great America, California's premier amusement park. After explaining quid pro quo, our principal, Mr. Reynolds, linked my ruthless behavior as reprehensible and deserving of expulsion. Two more words he would have to explain before my look of confusion would turn to tears of guilt and shame. Because we were approaching the end of the year, he would not expel me from school, but would suspend me (a term I was all too familiar with) and I would lose my privilege of joining my class on their end-of-year trip.

"Could I go with another class?" My filter-less mouth blurted out.

My habit of inserting humor in uncomfortable moments earned me an especially awful beating from Daddy that night.

Being suspended for two days on a Thursday meant I had a four-day weekend to recover from the WWE Smack Down I had secured from my embarrassing behavior. Brainwashed into believing I deserved it, I accepted the harsh punishment. I had crossed a line, but the truth was, I didn't know how to stop. I was so desperate for control in a life where I had none that trying my hand at bullying seemed like my only option.

With summer now upon me again, I had to find ways to stay out of sight and out of mind when Daddy was around and Mama was gone, taking care of the family business or running errands. That summer, however, I had turned eight and earned the delightful privilege of roaming the neighborhood until the streetlights came on, and I would learn to devour every minute of my newfound freedom. I spent my days outside, often running barefoot from sunrise to sundown, pretending I was like any other kid. I liked to think of myself as free, but freedom was an illusion.

Whenever Daddy had a slow day at work or came home early, his attention shifted to me. To give Mama a break, he would take me to run errands, which was code for going to one store or job site to pick up an item or complete a quick task that usually took minutes to complete. We spent the rest of the time on long drives to empty parking lots, far from any sign of life. Other than the occasional stray dog or cat, it was just us for miles. Daddy's "Special Time," as he would call it. A phrase I grew to detest. In the backseat of his truck, he tried, again and again, to force his way through the barrier between my legs, many times, leading to his inappropriately placed anger toward me as I would scream, yell, or cry out in agony. My absolute appropriate reaction to his absurd and inappropriate behavior would cause him to lash out at me and had even convinced me that somehow, I was a failure. I felt extremely conflicted about the activities I took part in during Daddy's alone time with me.

The lady at school had called that area between my legs my No-No spot, the place that no one should touch. Her words haunted me. I believed her, but what was I supposed to do when Daddy did the thing she taught was wrong? I felt torn between what I knew in my gut and what Daddy would continuously reassure me was okay to do only with him and no one could know.

He wanted to break something inside me I didn't fully understand yet, the only piece of me left that held onto some semblance of my innocence. Each time he failed to break me, his anger grew, and each time, I felt a strange sense of victory. But it was fleeting, as thoughts of being a failure lingered while shame coiled its breathtaking grip around me. Even when I was away from him, playing near the creek with the older kids, the weight of what was happening would follow me.

The big kids near the creek were my escape, my way of feeling brave even if I didn't belong. They would smoke things that smelled like a skunk had exploded, their laughter ringing out in bursts that echoed through the dusty summer air. They were older, cooler, and effortlessly intimidating. I craved their acceptance and the distraction they offered, even if it came with a fair share of ridicule. Crossing the creek on the makeshift rope swing was a rite of passage and expectation for any child who dare hang out in their part of the woods. I had dodged the expected requirement as long as I could, fading into the background day after day, but was called out. I immediately wanted to run and hide, but I knew that the only way I could return to the cool kids' club in the woods was to take this leap of faith or leap to my death.

The creek was wide and murky, and as I stood on its edge, my shoulder tense with fear. With ease, the other children jumped over it, their feet barely touching the muddy water as they laughed and shouted at each other. The edge loomed beneath me, and fear crawled up my spine as I wrapped my trembling hands around the scratchy rope, slick with sweat. My mouth was dry, and I swallowed hard.

"I'm not scared," I lied, my voice quivering slightly.

I forced a grin, hoping it made me look braver than I felt. But my heart pounded so hard I thought it might leap out of my chest. I stood there in perfect position to glide across if only my legs would take the leap and my scrawny arms could hold me. As hard as I tried to make myself jump, I hesitated, my legs rooted to the ground, paralyzed even as my insides screamed to just do it.

The older kids grew inpatient, and their once cheerful words of encouragement turned into stings of insults and taunts. Deep down, I knew that if I jumped and fell, I would never hear the end.

One of the older girls in line to go next rolled her eyes and muttered, "Figures. Little baby can't handle a simple jump."

Her words cut like a fiery blade but were on point. With my head down and my ego bruised, I slowly handed the rope to the next kid and bit my lip hard to cause pain and keep me from crying in front of everyone. I clenched my fists, trying to suppress the feeling of shame that crept up my spine and weaved my way through the group. I released my avalanche of emotions when I got out of the woods and was far enough away from any witnesses. My tank top absorbed the flood of tears the best it could. Refusing to share my emotions with a single soul, not even my mother, I took the long way home, allowing the summer heat an opportunity to dry my tears and my drenched tank top. I never returned to the creek in the woods that summer in Carmichael, California.

CHAPTER 5

BROKEN TRUST

LOOK AT THIS STUFF, isn't it neat? Wouldn't you think my collection's complete? Wouldn't you think I'm the girl, the girl who has everything? These opening lines from The Little Mermaid, my all-time favorite song in one of the most iconic classic movies, never failed to make me burst into song. Every time I hear or read these lyrics, I can't help but sing along. Ariel's rebellious curiosity and yearning for something more always struck a chord with me. Her character mirrored a part of me, resonating deep within my soul. She wasn't just a cartoon; she was a reflection of my own dreams and defiance. A mermaid who made me believe in the possibility of exploring new worlds beyond my own.

Swimming at Grandpa Brooks' house or a friend's pool was the highlight of my summer. I swam with my legs entwined together like a mermaid, my movements fluid and graceful. With every stroke, I sang my heart out, hoping to somehow will myself into becoming someone else. In my mind, I envisioned a magical transformation taking place. I'd bolt to the bottom of the pool, then with a powerful thrust; I would jut my body upward, gliding along the beams of sunlight that pierced through the water like shards of glass. I followed the radiant paths to the surface, imagining myself majestically breaking through the still waters, emerging as a true mermaid. In those moments, I wasn't just a girl playing pretend; I was Ariel, the Little Mermaid, transformed by the magic of my imagination.

California's record-shattering heat wave in the summer of 1987 was brutal. Each day dragged on as the merciless sun beat down on its victims. My mission to stay away from home from sunup to sundown required serious fine-tuning if I was to survive the searing heat. Without food, water, or shelter, I had to get creative to continue Operation Avoid Home. Strategic determination led me to the local park, a place teeming with potential allies. I spent hours playing with other children, searching for my next haven. My ability to make friends quickly became a lifeline, offering brief respite from the suffocating conditions. However, the cycle was harsh and unforgiving. I could integrate myself into a family's routine one moment, only to overstay my welcome the next. Because the stakes were so high, each day felt like a desperate dance of survival and evasion. The park became my battleground, where I waged a silent war against the heat and the looming dread of home. The dire necessity matched the intensity of my quest only to keep moving, keep adapting, and keep finding alternative places to seek refuge.

Meeting Grace Parker felt like a blessing. She and her family welcomed me into their home and seamlessly wove me into the fabric of their daily lives. I called her Gracie, and she embraced her nickname, as did her family, who also started calling her Gracie. Her home became a sanctuary, a place where I could spend the night on weekends and during the long summer days. I spent every free moment there, losing myself in the safety and comfort provided by her family. Her room became my room, her pool my pool, and her family my family. Gracie's house transformed into my personal refuge, much like Ariel's secret cave in The Little Mermaid, where she could truly be herself. It wasn't just a physical space; it was an emotional sanctuary where I felt protected and valued. Every moment I spent there was a reprieve from the fear and uncertainty that haunted me. Gracie's home wasn't just a safe house, it was a lifeline, a glimpse of what life could be like in a world where I was safe, loved, and free.

When the weather permitted, I could swim in their majestic pool, recreating every scene from The Little Mermaid. Their pool was enormous, with a diving board that became my launch pad for adventure. I would jump as high as I could, folding my tiny body into a tight ball and crashing into the water with a perfect cannonball. Every dive, every splash, felt like a desperate attempt to savor each moment, as if it might be my last chance to swim in Gracie's pool.

I swam with an intensity that bordered on obsession, barely stopping to eat or drink. Mrs. Parker had a strict rule: after eating, we had to sit out for thirty minutes to let our food digest. To avoid this enforced break, I often skipped meals, determined not to waste a single precious minute out of the water. I out-swam all the Parker children, often being the last one in the pool as they tired and retreated to the house for other activities.

I didn't mind being alone in the water; in fact, I preferred it. It was during those solitary swims that I could fully immerse myself in my imaginary world. I became Ariel, gliding through the water with effortless grace, my legs transforming into a powerful tail that propelled me through the cool depths. The pool became my ocean, a place where I could escape reality and embrace the freedom of my fantasies. Each stroke, each dive, was a moment of pure, unfiltered joy, a brief respite from the pain and fear that haunted my daily life.

I was always on my best behavior while dining with the Parkers, meticulously using all my manners to ensure I never jeopardized my invitation. I even forced myself to eat foods I detested, like liverwurst sandwiches. To this day, I do not know what liverwurst is exactly, but I can say with certainty that I never want to eat that revolting stuff again. At the Parkers, I found a sense of comfort and acceptance that had been foreign to me. I could be myself without fear of judgment or punishment. They welcomed me with open arms, treating me as one of their own.

One sunny Saturday during that scorching summer, Gracie's family excitedly prepared for a day on Folsom Lake, their boat primed for water skiing adventures. As they packed coolers and loaded gear, they casually invited me along.

Without a second thought, I blurted an enthusiastic, "Yes!"

Mrs. Parker, Gracie's mom, chuckled warmly, her hand covering her mouth as she nearly choked on her Pepsi in amusement. She gently reminded me, "Honey, you'll need to ask your mother first."

Frantically, I called Mama to ask permission. She agreed, but on one condition: I had to come home first to get a change of clothes. With a mix of excitement and relief, I rushed home to gather what I needed, my heart racing with anticipation for the adventure awaiting me on Folsom Lake with Gracie's family.

It was a whirlwind of excitement and nerves coursing through me as I dashed back to Mama's house, fueled by the prospect of joining

Gracie's family for a day out on the lake. Every pedal of my scooter thudded against the pavement with purpose, propelling me forward with a determination to make it back to Gracie's in record time. The wind whipped through my hair as I maneuvered through the familiar streets, my heart pounding with anticipation. Arriving home, I hurried inside to grab my change of clothes, a mix of relief and urgency pushing me to move faster. Moments later, I was back at Gracie's just as they were loading up their massive SUV. Mrs. Parker greeted me with a warm smile, and gently applied sunscreen to my arms and face before we embarked on our adventure.

Chatter and excitement filled the drive to Folsom Lake.

I sat in awe as we unloaded the boat and prepared for a day of water skiing. Lunchtime arrived swiftly, and we indulged in sandwiches, cold Canada Dry ginger ale, and crunchy Lay's potato chips on the boat deck. For me, it felt like stepping into a dream surrounded by good company; the sun warming my skin, and the shimmering lake stretching out before us. It was a slice of heaven I had only imagined until that day.

One by one, we took turns on the boat, each of us trying our hand at water skiing. I had never been on a boat before, let alone tried water skiing, but now it was my turn. Mr. Parker, with his reassuring smile, helped me strap into the giant skis and gently lowered me into the cool, welcoming water.

"Wait here while I take the slack out of the line," he instructed, his voice calm amidst the excitement.

I watched intently as Gracie's siblings, Lucas and Lily, effortlessly rose from the murky water, their skis slicing through the lake's surface with grace. It seemed easy enough. They made it look effortless, gliding around the lake as if they were born to ski. As I bobbed in the water, holding onto the handle, my heart raced with a mix of nerves and anticipation. The coolness of the lake swaddled me as I focused on Mr. Parker's instructions. This was my chance to prove myself, to experience something entirely new.

Bobbing up and down in the water, I waited with bated breath for the slack in the rope to tighten, signaling my moment to rise above the surface. The anticipation built, stirring a mix of excitement and nerves that churned in my stomach like a tempest at sea. When the rope tightened, it pulled me forward with a sudden jolt. I felt the exhilarating rush as my body rose, lifted by the tension in the line. For a fleeting moment, I was standing on the water, buoyed by a surge of adrenaline. My excitement, however, soon turned to panic as my legs wobbled under the unfamiliar weight and movement. Trying to stay upright, I lost my balance and tumbled forward, crashing onto my chest, skimming across the surface like a skipping stone.

The boat surged forward, dragging me mercilessly across the lake's surface. I clung desperately to the rope, arms stretched out, my grip tightening with every bounce and jerk. Waves crashed over me, plunging me under, only to thrust me back onto the surface like a rag doll tossed in a storm. Each plunge into the water left me gasping for air, disoriented and vulnerable. With every wave that washed over me, I struggled to maintain my grip, my body flailing as I fought against the unforgiving pull. Through the blur of water and spray, I strained to make out the figures on the boat. The Parker family's faces were a distant blur, their gestures and shouts lost in the wind's roar and the churn of the boat's engine.

After what felt like an eternity of being snatched and thrown like a toy, Mr. Parker's voice cut through the disarray like a megaphone through a storm. "Let go of the rope!" he shouted through a bullhorn, loud and clear.

Now, I wasn't exactly fluent in cursing back then, but in that heart-stopping moment, I blurted out, "Are you fucking kidding me?"

It was one of Daddy's go-to phrases, and it felt like the perfect response to the sheer absurdity of the situation. Of course, Mr. Parker couldn't hear my colorful response from across the lake, but maybe he sensed my panic or saw the terror in my eyes.

"The life jacket will keep you afloat!" he hollered, his voice amplified by the bullhorn. "We'll come back for you, but first you must let go of the rope."

Thank goodness for that booming voice and the clarity it brought, or else I might still be flopping around Folsom Lake. With a gulp of determination, I released my grip on the rope and let the life jacket do its job. As the boat circled back to retrieve me, I bobbed in the water like a bewildered buoy, grateful to be out of the whirlpool of panic and splashes. Looking back, that day on the lake marked my brief but memorable introduction into water skiing, along with my swift exit from the sport. For the rest of the afternoon, I admired the Parker family's athletic abilities on the water from the safety of the boat.

Mrs. Parker's warmth and kindness always covered me like a comforting blanket. One particular evening, as I stayed over, the usual routine of bedtime rituals unfolded. Mrs. Parker tucked me into the cozy top bunk bed, her soft touch a soothing balm to my restless spirit. It was at that moment, bathed in the soft glow of the bedside lamp, that I felt a surge of courage to share my inner turmoil with her. Lying there, staring at the ceiling while Mrs. Parker listened attentively, I cautiously confided in her about some of the strange and unsettling experiences that had been plaguing me. It was a risk, but in Mrs. Parker's presence, I felt a flicker of hope that she might understand, and that she might help me.

Her response was beyond comforting. She held my hand reassuringly, her eyes reflecting empathy and concern. She didn't dismiss my fears or brush them aside; instead, she promised to do whatever she could to support me. Her words were like a lifeline, offering a glimmer of hope in the darkness that had clouded my young life. That night, as I drifted off to sleep with a sense of cautious optimism, I couldn't help but wonder if I had found someone who could guide me through the storm. Her kindness had planted a seed of hope in my heart, and for the first time in a long while, I dared to believe that tomorrow might bring something better.

The following day, Mrs. Parker's unexpected announcement about my premature departure barely registered at first. I assumed it was a routine family visit to Gracie's grandparents, something that occasionally cut short my stay at their warm, welcoming home. Little did I know, behind the scenes, Mrs. Parker had made a call that morning, one that would alter my fragile sense of security.

Arriving home, the atmosphere shifted dramatically. It didn't take long to realize what had transpired while I was away. Mrs. Parker's call to my parents had unleashed a storm of disbelief and denial. My parents reassured Mrs. Parker of my safety, brushing off my accounts as fabrications crafted for attention. Mrs. Parker and my parents concluded I was spinning tales, seeking sympathy where there was none to be found. The fallout was swift and crushing. The once-open door to Gracie's house slammed shut, its warmth and safety suddenly out of reach. No longer welcome in their home, I found myself abruptly cut off from the refuge I had grown to cherish. The neighborhood park, where Gracie and I once played carefree for hours, became a silent reminder of lost companionship.

Not long after, the final blow fell with our family's move. Life in Carmichael, California abruptly ended, leaving behind the fleeting promise of stability that Mrs. Parker's kindness had briefly offered. As we packed up our belongings and prepared to embark on a new chapter, once again, uncertainty loomed large, mingled with a hint of anticipation for whatever lay ahead. Yet again, an unexplained move, rendering me totally confused. Leaving behind the familiar streets and faces of Carmichael marked the end of one chapter, but it also stirred a restless curiosity about the future. With each passing mile, I wondered where life's next adventure would lead, and whether I would ever find another Mrs. Parker along the way, someone who could see beyond the facade of denial while offering hope, understanding and acceptance once more.

"There are two kinds of pain in this world. The pain that hurts, and the pain that alters."
—Denzel Washington

PART 2
ALMOST NORMAL LIFE

CHAPTER 6

SWEET TEMPTATIONS, SOUR REALITIES

WE FREQUENTLY SPENT TIME at my mother's parents' home, with Grandma Marilyn and Mama's stepfather, Giovanni, but for me, he was simply Grandpa Gio. They were my two most favorite people in the world, and I felt like their favorite grandchild. The ride to their house was long and scenic, filled with trees, houses, and winding roads, but my excitement always outweighed the length of the drive. Staying with my grandparents a couple of weekends a month was a privilege I cherished. I would often beg my mother for more drop-off visits, yearning for the comfort and love I found at their home. My mother, however, said it was too much for Grandma, who was battling cancer and frequently ill. I didn't fully understand what that meant, other than cancer makes you lose your hair.

One day, as I walked out of Grandma and Grandpa's room holding Grandma's wig, she delicately removed it from my hands and explained that she lost her hair fighting cancer and that I was never to touch any of her wigs again. That was the extent of my cancer knowledge for many years. I hated her cancer, but for all the wrong reasons. Not because it made her violently ill after each chemotherapy treatment, and not because it would steal her from my life before I had the chance to learn how much I truly needed her, or because it would rob my children from ever knowing such a magnificent soul; I hated Grandma's cancer because it meant that I couldn't stay over more often, resulting in me having to be home when Daddy was there. It meant more time with him since he rarely worked weekends. One perk of owning your own business, he would often proclaim. Weekends were Daddy's opportunity to spend quality time with me, one-on-one time, as he played the role of a regular old father of the year.

Grandma and Grandpa had a beautiful home built on top of a hill in El Dorado County. The red clay dirt that filled their land was my imaginary stomping ground, a vast playground where I could let my imagination run wild. I explored every inch of their property, including the forbidden hill behind their home that led to a retaining wall with a dangerous drop-off.

Being the rebellious child I was, this wall was merely a challenge. Every visit was an opportunity to see how far I could scoot down before risking a fall to my death. My last visit to the forbidden wall included me scaring the crap out of myself, going down way too far and not knowing if I could climb back up. Crying out for help, however, was never an option. Although I was confident in Grandpa's ability to rescue me, I was also certain that the beating waiting for me at home would be worse than plummeting off the cliff. Covered in red clay, I frantically dug my way back up, using my hands to claw into the hill and forcing my feet to create footholds. Each desperate movement was driven by fear, but I finally reached safety. That harrowing experience was enough to redirect my energy to exploring other, less life-threatening adventures.

On a subsequent visit, my outdoor play shifted to climbing the fence to explore the nearby water treatment facility. The "Keep Out" sign offered the perfect boost needed to reach the top of the fence. Once I had my fill of trespassing, I began collecting various twigs and sticks. These natural treasures became the materials for my next masterpiece: a marvelous picture frame I glued together to showcase my latest artwork. The following day, when my mother collected me, I intended to give her the framed masterpiece.

The next morning, I woke up with a face so swollen I could barely open my eyes. My entire body itched like crazy, and a red rash covered every inch of my skin, yes, even my little butt cheeks. I stumbled my way to my grandparents, scratching all the way.

Before I could speak, Grandpa lowered his newspaper, shook his head, and announced, "Looks like Chris has poison oak."

"I didn't touch the leaves of three!" I protested immediately.

Grandpa had taught me the rhyme a while back: "Leaves of three, let them be." Apparently, I had missed that crucial detail while playing outside the day before. Grandpa had me show him where I'd collected the twigs and sticks, and sure enough, it was poison oak.

I wailed, "But there were no leaves!"

Grandpa patted me on the head and explained, "I know, sweetie, but unfortunately, the plant can still be poisonous even when the leaves die off. The oils from the plant can cause an allergic reaction."

As if having an allergic reaction all over my body wasn't bad enough, I was devastated when Grandma broke the dreadful news that we would have to throw away my picture frame and artwork since they were glued together. I cried and pleaded to save my art. Grandpa strolled into the kitchen with his camera, and I immediately thought, why would he want to take a picture of me? I look horrible!

"Chris, how about I take a picture of your artwork before we have to dispose of it?" Grandpa suggested.

"Yes, yes, please! I would like that very much," I replied, relieved.

While Grandpa photographed my beloved masterpiece, Grandma began lathering me up with calamine lotion, wearing latex gloves. My artwork would remain memorable, even if destined for the trash, despite my appearance as a spotted pink ghost.

Oh, how I digress. Back to this visit, my near-death cliff-plummeting experience ended when I heard the familiar, soothing voice of my grandmother calling me inside to get cleaned up for dinner. She had learned long ago that I was not one of those children who could simply come inside and wash their hands before taking a seat on her custom-upholstered dining chairs. She knew all too well that I would need to wash thoroughly and change my clothes before being allowed near any of her pristine furniture.

I bounded up the stairs to the expansive porch, but before I could dart inside and risk tarnishing Grandma's immaculate carpet, a routine was in order. Not only did I need to take off my shoes and socks, but after my adventurous afternoon on the cliff, I was told to strip down to my underwear right there on the porch. Since this was typical after my outdoor adventures, I didn't think twice about standing there in the My Little Pony underwear Daddy and I found during a late-night Goodwill run.

Grandma insisted I take a shower rather than my usual bath, explaining that I was far too filthy to stew in my bathwater. After a whirlwind shower that somehow left my hair still dry, I dressed and headed to dinner. As I took my seat, a familiar aroma made me grin from ear to ear. Grandma made my favorite tuna casserole with peas. Grandma and Grandpa fell silent for a moment as they glanced my way, making me briefly anxious, until Grandma chuckled warmly and Grandpa shook his head. He informed me that my mother was going to insist on another bath once I got home that evening. Glancing down, I noticed streaks of red clay still clinging to my slender arms. We shared a laugh over this and then delved into our meal. Dining early at my grandparent's meant there was always room for a snack before bedtime, which suited me perfectly as I was usually hungry again by then.

Midway through our delicious dinner, a knock at the door and my mother's voice announcing her arrival interrupted us. A mix of excitement to see her and dread at the thought of leaving washed over me. She joined us for the rest of the meal, and we left shortly after, carrying with us the warmth of the evening and the lingering laughter.

Our car ride started like countless others, Mama belting out whatever hit song was playing on the radio, her voice effortlessly filling the car. I sat quietly in back behind the passenger seat, watching her in awe and occasionally singing along if I knew the song. I was completely mesmerized by the beauty and warmth of her voice. Singing had always been her joy, and she had a way of making even the saddest songs sound comforting. I could have listened to her sing for hours, as her voice filled the air, forgetting the world outside for just a little while.

About twenty minutes into our hour-long drive home, we made a routine stop at the local AM/PM gas station. As the car screeched to a halt, Mama's previously warm, joyful voice turned stern as she launched into her familiar mantra: "Touch nothing, don't ask for anything. We're just getting gas and using the restroom."

Yet, as I trailed behind her into the brightly lit store, the shelves bursting with temptations, my young, undiagnosed ADHD mind went into overdrive. I launched into my usual pleas for gum, candy, toys, and an Icee.

My insatiable desire for every brightly packaged candy, all strategically placed at eye level, was enough to fray my mother's last nerve.

She bent down, gripped my bicep firmly, and sternly reminded me, "We're here to get gas and use the restroom, that's it!"

While she paid for the gas, I wandered down the candy aisle, my eyes darting between the treats within reach and the adults at the register. Seizing a moment of distraction, I quickly palmed a yellow pack of Juicy Fruit gum and, with the stealth of a trained ninja, slipped it into the pocket of my purple trench coat. There was just one problem: a gaping tear inside my pocket let my ill-gotten prize slip into the unreachable depths of my coat lining.

Back in the van, I frantically rummaged through my pocket, fingers probing the frayed material in a desperate search for the gum.

My unusual fidgeting caught my mother's attention, prompting her to ask, "Tina, what are you doing?"

I froze and replied suspiciously, "Nothing!"

My unconvincing demeanor instantly switched her into detective mode. She dove into my pocket as I clutched the bottom of my coat, betraying the location of the hidden gum. With a practiced motion, she extracted the 25¢ pack of gum through the hole in my pocket.

I was caught. Mama paused, gum in hand, and staring at me in disbelief. Her odd calmness instantly sent a wave of anxiety trickling through my body. What was she going to do? Would she tell Daddy, guaranteeing a harsh punishment, or might she, just maybe, keep this between us? Frozen with fear, I stared at the untied shoelaces of my dirty white Converse shoes, now stained a deep red from the clay dirt, as dread of the unknown settled heavily upon me.

The click of the gas pump snapped me from my dread. My mother calmly instructed, "Come with me."

Confused and terrified, I stumbled behind her back into the store. My mind raced through every scenario as we stood in line. Perhaps she had forgotten my theft, merely waiting to get a receipt. That had to be it. As we approached the counter, she tugged my hand forward.

Expecting to hear her ask for a receipt, I was unprepared when she looked down at me and commanded in an unfamiliar authoritative tone,

"Go ahead. Tell him what you did."

Rooted to the spot, my abdomen clenched like a fist as I stood there frozen. I avoided her gaze and faced the attendant.

"Christina Jeanine Brooks!" she snapped. "Tell this gentleman what you did."

Looking down, I mumbled, "I got a piece of gum."

"No, you stole a pack of gum," she corrected firmly.

With a trembling voice, I confessed, "Um, I... I stole a pack of gum."

As my mother spoke with the clerk, my attention faded to the grimy floor tiles, wishing for this moment to end. A nudge from my mother brought me back, as she insisted, "Apologize for stealing the gum."

"I'm sorry I stole the pack of gum, and I won't do it again. I promise." I added "I promise," to mitigate the impending consequences.

The attendant, unimpressed, leaned down and asked gruffly if he should call the police. His breath was heavy with the stench of cigarettes and decay.

Recoiling, I pleaded, "No! Please don't tell the police on me."

His expression remained stony as he dismissed me with a chastising, "Don't do it again."

Sobbing, I repeated my apologies, and with one last apology from my mother to the attendant, we left the store, a heavy silence falling between us as we returned to the car.

On the ride home, Mama was unusually quiet. There was no singing, no cheerful voice to get lost in. She reached over and turned the radio off completely, leaving behind a heavy, awkward silence. It filled the car like a thick fog, as if even the air was holding its breath. I stole glances at her, sensing she was somewhere far away, lost deep in thought, and in that moment, the space between us felt wider than the road ahead.

I sat in silence, my mind consumed with fear about what would happen when Daddy found out. When we arrived, I heard my parents talking in the kitchen. Seizing the moment, I tiptoed to my room, hoping they might forget about me if I stayed quiet. Hope quickly faded as my towering, two-hundred-and-fifty-pound father burst into my room. In one swift motion, he lifted me from my bed and delivered a series of harsh spanks to my body. His blows were indiscriminate, landing heavily not just on my bottom but across my back, legs, and torso as well.

My frantic attempts to dodge each hit, flopping and twisting like a fish out of water, only made matters worse.

As my cries grew louder, he would snarl with a tone that seemed almost amused, "I'll give you something to cry about!"

It was another one of those baffling adult phrases that made no sense. After what felt like forever, the beating ceased. I thought it was time for my bedtime snack and another attempt at a bath. Sadly, I was mistaken.

"Go to bed!" he bellowed.

"But what about my snack? I'm hungry," I sobbed.

"No, you're not," he retorted sharply. "Go to bed!"

This wasn't the first time I'd gone to bed hungry because of my misbehavior, and it wouldn't be the last.

CHAPTER 7

YEARNING FOR SAFETY

FROM THE OUTSIDE, OUR family looked like any other, but within our four walls, a complex and isolating reality unfolded daily. My much younger siblings, Michael and Angela, shared a bond with Daddy that was only a dream for me. He treasured and doted on them, showering them with the warmth I desperately craved. Their laughter filled the house, untouched by the shadows that clung to me. I watched from the sidelines as he ruffled Michael's hair or kissed Angela's cheek, his face soft and filled with the love for which I ached. With me, his demeanor would change. His expression was like stone, filled with something colder and sharper. From as young as I could remember, I sensed something different about my place in the family. For my brother and sister, he was Daddy, a word that meant safety, laughter, and pride. However, he treated me as if I owed him money, making me endure his scorn, harsh reprimands, and severe beatings; when no one was watching, he used me for his twisted sexual pleasure. "Secret Time" was the only non-violent attention I received from Daddy. I grew to expect it, although I never liked it and felt wrong taking part in it. It was better than being his punching bag; I supposed.

I'd often catch myself in the mirror, studying my features, searching for something on my face that looked like his, hoping to find some resemblance that would explain why he was my father. The only thing we shared was a small gap between our two front teeth. Everything else felt foreign. Deep down, I hoped he wasn't my real dad, that he couldn't be. Such treatment of a child by a father was unfathomable. Why did I feel like an outsider in my family? Why did he have such softness for Michael and Angela, and only coldness and anger for me?

As I navigated these turbulent waters, I sought refuge in my mother's old photo albums, scanning every faded face, every grainy memory for a clue, hoping to piece together the fragments of my past. Then, I found him, a tall, scrawny white guy with long blond hair in her prom picture. There was something about his crooked smile and friendly eyes that contrasted with the stern, unforgiving gaze of the man currently raising me that made my heart race. This had to be my real dad. He became a symbol of hope, a knight destined to rescue me from my nightmarish reality. I clung to this fantasy with fervent longing, believing that someday this man would come to claim me, to explain his absence and end my suffering. Frequently, I sat by the enormous living room window of our Elk Grove house. I'd watch distant cars go by, each one potentially him. I pictured him showing up at our front door. In my mind, he was larger than life, a hero, someone who would see me as special. I'd imagine him reaching down, lifting me up into his arms, telling me he'd been looking for me all along.

My fantasy was the only thing that kept me going for some days. It was my secret escape, a small glimmer of hope. I would stare at that photo, whispering to it like a friend, like a father who could hear my pain. But every morning, I'd wake up, and he'd still be just a photo, a fading face in a dusty album. Daddy would still be there, cold and distant until he wasn't. When I'd question Mama about my real father, she'd brush me off.

"Curtis is your father, Tina," she'd insist, her voice a wall I couldn't climb.

I'd argue until the words blurred into tears, but she'd stay silent, like she was guarding a secret that was meant to stay buried. The harder I tried to pry open that door, the more locked out I felt.

"Why doesn't he love me like Michael and Angela? Why am I different?"

Her response would cut deep. "Your behavior determines how you're treated."

A phrase I heard Daddy shout frequently as his justification when Mama attempted to stick up for me, during many of their late-night fights starring me, the terrible child. It was a response that stung with its implication of inadequacy. Not only had Daddy convinced Mama I deserved his harsh ways, I believed it as well. I wondered if she would still believe that if she knew what he did to me during our "Secret Time." I couldn't tell her; the shame and confusion were too much and by this time Daddy had led me to believe he would hurt Mama if I ever shared our secret with anyone.

Reality is seldom like the dreams of a child. As the fantasy of my real father faded, it left a void that was impossible to fill. I came to realize that no one was coming to save me. I was utterly alone. The painful truth settled heavily in my chest, forcing me to reckon with the fact that I had to find a way to survive on my own. The arguments with Mama intensified, leaving me with more questions than answers, and every day I drifted further from the family for which I longed. In my heart, I was certain this man I called Daddy was not my father. His name was Curtis, and that was all he would ever be to me.

Not until much later did I comprehend that the same man who made my life a living hell had trapped Mama in her own nightmare. She couldn't protect me because she could barely protect herself. When I watched her shrink under his gaze, flinch at his slightest movement, I saw the brokenness in her that mirrored my own. She had scars too, hidden beneath her silence and submission. The scars created by Daddy accompanied the scars she had received as a child and had kept hidden. There was an indescribable sorrow in her eyes. Over the years, she had mastered the art of hiding her pain from the rest of the world. I could see it. Now and then, the pain was too much to bear, and she could no longer hide it. I learned that sometimes the people who should protect us are just as powerless as we are. Through it all, I held onto a glimmer of hope, even if it was dim, even if no one would be my hero. I clung to the possibility that I could somehow save myself and Mama from this tyrant of a man. It was a fragile belief, but it was all I had. The thought of one day breaking free, of no longer being defined by his cruelty, was enough to keep me going.

CHAPTER 8

THE CRY UNHEARD

LIKE MANY OF MY menacing experiences with Daddy, this afternoon's errands also became unpleasant. As usual, a quick stop at the local hardware store turned into an anxiously long drive to an unknown destination. We never visited one place too many times to not bring attention to ourselves, I suppose. Entering the abandoned parking lot adorned with a once vibrant, now rusted sign of the old Family Fun Center loomed over us, tilted slightly, as if bowing under the weight of its own abandonment. It stood as a ghostly reminder of happier times. Times that weren't mine to remember but belonged to other children, other families, who came here for joy, laughter, and games. As Daddy's old truck rumbled into the empty parking lot, I couldn't help the foolish flicker of hope that sparked in my chest. Maybe this time, I whispered under my breath. Maybe this time, we really were here for fun. Bumper cars. Skee ball. Greasy, dripping slices of pizza. I could almost taste it, feel the vibrations of a collision in bumper cars, hear the satisfying clunk of a Skee ball landing in the 100-point slot. My eyes darted to the cracked pavement, and the forgotten prizes locked inside the dusty arcade, and for one fleeting second, I let myself believe.

Daddy didn't get out of the car to open the doors of the fun center. Instead, he parked in a far corner, out of sight, yet able to see if anyone approached from the highway. The hope that bubbled in my chest sank like a stone, crashing down into a pit of dread. I knew this routine, this sick game disguised under the pretense of family time. Fun wasn't why we were here. It was never fun for me.

"Come here," Daddy said, his voice soft but threatening, like the low rumble of a storm cloud.

I froze, my small fingers digging into the cracked fabric of the seat, willing my body to disappear, to blend into the background. But it did not work. It never did. Forcing myself to move, I slowly scooted over, my limbs sluggish. Knowing that resistance would only make things worse, I forced my body to ignore my mind's desperate plea to open the door and run somewhere, anywhere else, but here. As I complied, I let my mind drift far, far away, constructing a protective barrier that numbed me to what was to come next. It was a dissociative dance I had perfected over time, a shield that didn't stop the pain but at least dulled its edge.

Interrupted by the introduction of a new form of torture, I was unable to remain focused in my mind's arena of safety. Handing me a number two pencil from the glove box, Daddy instructed me to insert the used writing utensil into my special spot, as he called it. Frozen in a state of utter confusion, my facial expressions spoke words my mouth could not convey. He assured me that this would help me get rid of the piece of skin that was stopping me from making him happy, insinuating that I was the one with the problem. Gaslighting at its finest! As he coached me through this awkward, not to mention extremely unsanitary act of perversion, tears flooded my cheeks with every failed attempt. Between my defiant outbursts of pain and my failure to complete this seemingly simple task, I upset Daddy. My failure felt bittersweet; although I desperately wanted to please Daddy and join the loved children's club, I grew to prefer his physical abuse over his sexual abuse. So, making him angry, even though that was not my intention, was a better outcome than the acts that would have followed had I had been successful in defiling my body. We drove home in silence; the car filled with the suffocating weight of unspoken words. My eyes fixed on the horizon, where the sky bled into shades of crimson and gold.

As soon as we stopped in the driveway, I bolted from the truck and retreated to my usual spot in the giant magnolia tree that towered over our front yard. That massive tree became one of my frequent hiding spots, offering an array of endless challenges. With each visit I would climb one branch higher than before with a goal of climbing high enough and far out on the limb that hovered next to the roof, hoping that one day I would summon the courage to make the leap from the giant tree to rooftop, never considering the return leap to the tree. My outdoor adventures, as usual, ended with the familiar hum of the streetlights turning on.

While impatiently waiting for dinner, I played in the TV room, carefully constructing my tower of blocks, meticulously stacking one after another until I was standing and crafting a tower taller than me. Suddenly, my little brother, Michael, swept in like the highly trained ninja he was, knocking down my tower with the proud grin only a four-year-old could possess. His laughter triggered an eruption of anger, causing me to lash out. My outburst caught Daddy's attention. After consoling his son, his attention quickly turned to me in the pursuit of justice. Daddy's eyes narrowed and his voice became hard and raspy with a force of vengeance behind it. I knew what was coming and braced myself for the blows. Before he could finish his thrashing, Mama intervened, only fueling his rage. He turned his attention to her.

Unable to accept his treatment of Mama, I stepped in, redirecting his attention back to me as I had practiced in previous fights, always resulting in success. Feeling proud of my ability to act as a tiny shield, I received each hit, every slap and all the harsh insults, like a badge of honor, until I could no longer absorb another one. When the pain became unbearable, I darted out of the front door and into the street.

"Help!" I screamed, my voice cracking under the weight of my terror.

My head on a swivel, searching for anyone. My small frame illuminated only by the streetlight next to our house. A couple pushing a stroller was passing by, their eyes meeting mine. For a split second, hope flared. They paused, their expressions unreadable, and I thought, *This is it. Someone's going to save me.* The shatter of my heart left me buckled over in terror as they looked away and increased the speed of their leisure walk.

I crumbled, the fight leaving my body, and collapsed onto the asphalt, still warm from the summer's heat. Loose rocks dug into my knees as I hysterically bawled: Mama came out, her face pale, and her eyes swollen with sorrow. She gathered me in her arms, whispering hollow comforts until my sobs quieted. I let her lead me back into the house, the warmth of her touch clashing with the cold reality that she couldn't protect herself or me, not from him, not from this.

In my room, I sat hunched on the edge of the bed. My eyes grew heavy and fewer tears slipped down my cheeks. I welcomed the idea of rest. No longer concerned with dinner or dessert, I started to lie down when the door burst open and Daddy stormed in. I sat back up on the edge of my bed in fear, bracing myself for another round with the heavyweight champ. Without a word, he stormed over and kicked me hard in my left shin; the force knocking me backward. My shin was no match for his steel toe cowboy boots that ripped through layers of skin like a hot knife through butter. Mesmerized by the shiny flap of flesh that hung grotesquely, I stared in shock as my brain took a moment to register what had just happened. When it did, it felt like fire. As he left, the door slammed, sealing me back in my world of silent suffering.

I gawked at the injury, the blood gushing down my leg. Once his footsteps faded, I stumbled to the bathroom across the hall. I slowly closed the door and sat on the toilet, examining the insides of my wound. The unzipped section of my shin revealed a shiny, pear-like material that didn't bleed; only the surrounding skin bled. Despite the amount of pain I was in, it looked cool. I'd never seen the inside of a leg before. I wrapped Mama's decorative hand towel around my leg to stop the bleeding. My growing curiosity thwarted my failed attempts to stop the bleeding. I repeatedly pulled back the skin flap to take a peek at what I now believed all my insides looked like. As my exhaustion set in and I became overrun with aches and pains, I carefully hobbled back to bed with my makeshift toilet paper bandage wrapped in a bloody hand towel.

Curled up in bed, I cried out loud for Mama until she came in and then I really turned on the waterworks so she would do something about my pain and that mean old man. She unwrapped my poor attempt of a bandage, exposing my mangled shin. I knew for certain that she would avenge me now. Unlike the things he did during our times alone, this was no secret, and she knew what he did. Surely, she would make him pay. Mama cleaned my leg and sprayed it with antiseptic spray that felt like fire and then bandaged it up.

With tear-filled desperate eyes, Mama reluctantly whimpered, "Tina, you know what happens when he gets angry."

Stunned by her words, something in me hardened. No one was coming to help. Not the couple in the street, not the neighbors, not a single soul; not even Mama could make him change. I could no longer hope for a savior. I was alone, my strength insufficient to face the beast. Relinquishing hope was my only option for survival in this house.

Feeling defeated, I cradled my pillow and during my tears, I must have fallen asleep. We never went to see a doctor about my leg. Looking back, I'm certain stitches or medical glue would have been an appropriate medical solution. Yet with the health care needed, too many questions would come. Questions regarding the cause of this injury and why we delayed going to the ER. Perhaps that's the reason we didn't get help. Mama cleaned my shin each day and the chunk of skin eventually scabbed up and fell off. I was never a good patient, though; I picked at my wound and often made it bleed and am sure that did not help, but it was the coolest thing I had ever seen. How many children get to see the inside of their body? The physical wound eventually healed, leaving a quarter size divot in my left shin. The emotional wound never healed. I just put it in a box on the back shelf of my mind. Every so often, someone would notice my scar and inquire how I did that to myself. In that moment, I would replay the night that my shin was forever scarred by the man who was supposed to be my father, my protector, my hero, and the internal wound would be ripped back open, oozing the warm, red blood of pain.

CHAPTER 9

STRANGERS IN FAMILIAR PLACES

FOR A BRIEF SEASON, my family and I lived with Daddy's parents, Grandma Mildred and Grandpa Howard in Sacramento, in their second home connected to their flourishing dental practice. It was a peculiar property, a combination of professional and personal spaces, filled with the strange inconsistencies that life presents. The house sat behind the clinic, separated only by a narrow walkway. Across the street, a massive golf course spread out in lush greens, and wayward golf balls often found their way into our backyard, rolling down to the creek where I spent most of my free time.

If I wasn't knee-deep in muddy waters, chasing crawdads and getting my fingers sliced up by their sharp claws, I was hustling. I'd collect the abandoned golf balls. Each one felt like a treasure. After I scrubbed them until they gleamed, I'd load them into my little red wagon, and wheel through the neighborhood, selling them to local golfers. Even at eight years old, I took pride in earning money, however small the amount. Each dollar felt like a symbol of independence, a rare freedom in a life where so little was under my control.

Starting school that year should have been exciting, but my homemade haircut crushed my confidence. Mama resorted to the "Big Chop" after growing exhausted from dealing with too many bouts with lice and my stubborn refusal to brush my tangled rat's nest of hair. The kids at school didn't let me forget it. Paired with my giant buck teeth and awkwardly short hair that made me look like a boy, I became a target for ridicule. My heart ached with the sting of cruel laughter and taunts, adding another layer to the mountain of insecurities and self-doubt I carried.

At home, there was a different cruelty. Like every house we lived in, Daddy wasted no time establishing a new hiding spot for his twisted desires. The basement was creepy, filled with relics of my grandparents' past lives. Dusty poker tables and boxes of forgotten keepsakes littered the musty, green, outdated carpet. Black widow spiders spun their webs in every dark corner and crevice, and while most kids would have been terrified, I almost welcomed the idea of a spider bite if it meant avoiding Daddy's filthy, suffocating touch. His abuses grew more sinister over time, and at such a young age, I had almost mastered the art of dissociating, retreating into my mind to escape the horror of the moment.

Yet, amidst the mayhem, there were flickers of light, treasured moments that kept me going. Grandpa Howard and Grandma Mildred owned a sprawling estate in Grass Valley we called The Meadows, and as a child, I both dreaded and longed for our visits there. The property was a wonderland with endless woods, countless bedrooms, spiral staircases, and wide-open spaces where I could run free.

Grandma Mildred showered my brother and sister with the unconditional warmth for which I longed. Her two-arm hugs for them were full of love and reassurance, while I was often met with a cold side hug, an obligatory, almost begrudging gesture that barely made contact.

Grandpa Howard had a gentler spirit. His kind eyes and polite pats on the head hinted at some understanding of the pain I carried, though he never crossed the boundary Grandma Mildred set. I knew he was trying, but his affection felt like a whisper of comfort in a storm of rejection. It was a strange thing, to feel like an unwanted guest among the family, to understand that the love they gave my siblings so freely would never be mine.

Still, I found joy in the little things. Holidays were the best times at the estate. Easter brought epic egg hunts that stretched across the vast property. My cousins and I would decorate eggs for hours, giggling and making a mess so the adults could hide them in a grand game of search and discovery. We'd race through the fields, laughing as we found egg after egg, only for the adults to reclaim them later to make deviled eggs and incorporate our once claimed prizes into potato salad. Occasionally, there were plastic eggs filled with candy, and those we got to keep. The joy of those moments made me feel almost normal, if only for a little while.

But the joy was fleeting, holidays ended, family left, and The Meadows grew quiet. That's when Daddy found ways to be alone with me again, disguising his intentions as "Father-Daughter Quality Time." He'd take me on ATV rides through the woods, leading me to abandoned shacks and empty trailers scattered across the property. I'd hold on to a naive hope, and let myself believe that maybe, this time, it would just be a fun adventure. Yet, it was never different.

The rides home from The Meadows were another battleground. One night, my legs ached terribly with what the doctors called growing pains. An intense throbbing pain, which no amount of rubbing or repositioning could ease. My whining quickly wore on Daddy's already thin patience, and no matter how many times Daddy threatened to give me something to cry about, it didn't work that night. I couldn't stop; the pain was consuming me. Finally, he snapped. The van swerved violently to the side of the road, our bodies jerking forward as he slammed on the brakes. He jumped out, fury in his eyes, yanked open the sliding door, and delivered his infamous "Knuckle Sandwich" to my thigh. A forceful punch, delivered with his middle knuckle protruding out, intensifying the impact of each strike. Every punch, a bolt of lightning that left me gasping in pain.

"Now, shut the fuck up," he seethed, slamming the door shut.

Mama tried to comfort me, promising medicine, as my sobs turned into quiet, defeated whimpers.

After many ignored pleas by Mama for Daddy to stop at the pharmacy, he eventually relented. Mama rubbed Absorbine Jr. into my bruised, aching legs. The burning sensation of the pain-relief liquid was a minor comfort, one of the countless bottles we'd gone through during my bouts of growing pains. Yet the physical ache was nothing compared to the emotional wounds left by feeling like an outsider, even in my family.

I didn't yet understand that my exclusion stemmed from the secret shame of being Daddy's biracial stepdaughter. Instead, I internalized every sideways glance and cold shoulder, convinced it was my fault. I carried the weight of believing I was inherently flawed, that something inside me was so broken or unlovable that ridicule, neglect, and rejection were what I deserved. The shame seeped into every part of my young identity, whispering lies about my worth until I could no longer separate lies from truth.

My maternal Grandmother Marilyn and step Grandfather Gio were the rare, precious exceptions in my life. Their love was a balm, soothing some of the deep, invisible wounds I carried. My childhood experience of unconditional love was centered on them. Grandma Marilyn's hugs enveloped me like a warm, protective blanket, her laughter a reminder that joy still had a place in my world. Grandpa Gio, with his patient wisdom and gentle presence, made me feel seen in a way I desperately needed. Their affection was abundant, pouring over me like a lifeline, momentarily breaking the spell of worthlessness I often felt. Their love, however, as powerful as it was, couldn't entirely shield me from the pain inflicted by others or erase the deep-seated belief that I was unworthy.

Those emotionally distant interactions with family members who should have loved me but kept me at arm's length shaped how I perceived relationships for years to come. Rejection became a familiar sting, a shadow that followed me into every new encounter. I craved validation like a thirst I couldn't quench, constantly striving to prove my worth to a world that I believed would never fully accept me. My childhood experiences planted seeds of self-doubt that would grow tangled and stubborn, wrapping around my heart and mind, taking decades to untangle. I became a "People Pleaser," molding myself to fit other's expectations, always trying to earn love I never believed I deserved.

Deep down, beneath the layers of trauma and scars, there remained a small, resilient part of me that refused to be extinguished. A flicker of hope, a stubborn ember, clung to the belief that love didn't always have to be earned, that somewhere out there was a place where I could be accepted just as I was. Even in the darkest moments, when the weight of rejection threatened to crush me, I kept that ember alive. It reminded me that perhaps, one day, I would find a place where I belonged, where love would be freely given, and where I could finally shed the burden of feeling like an outsider.

CHAPTER 10

WRESTLING WITH SHADOWS

AS A CHILD, THERE was a recurring nightmare that played out in the waking hours of my life. When Mama was away or often when she was in the shower, Daddy, with his towering frame and rough hands, would smother me. Lying on top of me, fully clothed, he would grind his body against mine. My lungs burned with the desperate need for air under his weight. The sensation of his calloused palm over my face, his giant frame crushing me, left an indelible mark on my psyche. Each time, I fought silently, the muffled screams trapped within me echoing in my mind long after he relented. These moments seared a deep-seated fear into my soul, a claustrophobia that shadowed my every move.

Years down the road, I found myself in the military, surrounded by a new family. Trust, shared experiences, and a tough exterior hiding inner weakness created camaraderie among the soldiers. Part of our training and bonding involved wrestling and grappling exercises meant to build strength and resilience, and to prepare us for hand-to-hand combat. For most, it was just another drill, another chance to prove themselves. For me, it was a battlefield of a different kind.

I remember a day of training like no other. The sun was blazing, casting a harsh light on the wrestling mat where we sparred during hand to hand combat training. My opponent, a fellow soldier named Specialist Cane, was someone I trusted. Yet trust didn't matter when the past came roaring back. In the heat of the match, he pinned me down, his weight pressing into my chest, his arm across my throat. Instantly, I was no longer in combative training. I was back in that small, suffocating space, under the crushing weight of Daddy. Panic set in like a wildfire. My vision blurred, and all I could feel was that familiar, paralyzing terror. I thrashed wildly, my breaths coming in ragged, desperate gasps. The rational part of my mind knew where I was, but the wounded child within me was drowning, reliving those horrific moments. The match ended abruptly as our instructor pulled Specialist Cane off me, recognizing the signs of my distress. I lay there, gasping for air, my body trembling uncontrollably. It was more than just physical exhaustion; it was the weight of years of unhealed trauma crashing down on me. My comrades looked at me with concern and confusion, but how could they understand the depth of what I was experiencing? I wasn't even fully aware of it myself. How could they know that each pin, each hold, was like reopening a wound that had never healed?

That day was a turning point for me. It became painfully clear that the past, no matter how deeply buried, would resurface with a vengeance and without notice. My claustrophobia wasn't just a fear of tight spaces; it was a visceral reaction to being overpowered and helpless, a reminder of the powerlessness of my childhood.

Later that evening, I sat alone in my barracks room, the events of the day replaying in my mind. Lost in thought, I heard Corporal Paris, one of the most respected and experienced junior soldiers in our unit, knock at my door.

I froze in silence, hoping whoever it was would leave until she announced, "I know you are in there. I just saw your roommate and I'm not leaving until you hear me out."

Having worked with Corporal Paris frequently, I knew she meant what she said and would not leave easily.

Reluctantly, I let her in.

"I saw what happened out there today," she said. "You looked like you were fighting more than just Specialist Cane. Want to talk about it?"

"Not really," I responded, sitting in the corner of my bed against the wall, avoiding eye contact and holding back my tears of shame.

She shared a personal story about an experience where overwhelming memories caused her to emotionally break down and cry in front of many of her comrades and superiors during a heated interaction with a supervisor. She explained how something the supervisor said triggered a terrible memory from her past marriage and brought her back to that moment when her ex-husband verbally and physically assaulted her. Her calm demeanor and transparency created a space where I felt I could do the same. She had a quiet wisdom about her, a calm presence that made me feel safe. I hesitated, but there was something about her that encouraged honesty.

"My stepfather used to smother me. When Specialist Cane pinned me down, it all came flooding back. I couldn't breathe. I felt like I was back there, a kid again, helpless."

For the first time, other than seeing a couple therapists while in foster care, whom I did not trust, I spoke about some of my childhood. Corporal Paris listened intently, her eyes never leaving mine.

Waiting for my pause, she interjected, "Triggers can be powerful. They can bring the past crashing into the present, but recognizing them is the first step toward dealing with them."

We talked long into the night. I confided in her about my experiences with physical and sexual abuse and some of my battles within the foster care system. She helped me understand that my reaction wasn't a sign of weakness, but a natural response to trauma. She encouraged me to seek counseling, to face these memories head-on rather than letting them control me. Most importantly, she made me feel understood, showing me that even the strongest among us have internal battles. It was an arduous journey, confronting those memories and working through the trauma, but it was necessary.

That evening was pivotal, yet despite the breakthrough, I struggled with deep-seated trust issues toward my previous therapist and initially brushed aside her advice to pursue further therapy. I had convinced myself that I had overcome my trauma. However, several years later, a playful innocent wrestling match with my older brother, Lewis, painfully underscored that my struggles were far from resolved. During the match, being pinned down triggered a profoundly familiar sense of panic. In a flurry of fear and anger, I reacted violently, kicking and punching wildly, culminating in a forceful kick to Lewis' ear that left him shocked and kneeling in pain. This alarming reaction was a stark reminder of the profound issues still simmering beneath my facade of bravado.

Realizing the gravity of my unaddressed trauma, I acknowledged that serious, sustained effort would be required to truly confront and heal from my past. I reluctantly began therapy, embarking on a challenging but necessary journey to confront and work through the shadows of my childhood trauma. This marked the beginning of a decade-long intensive healing process that engaged a team of clergy, mental health professionals, numerous inpatient stays, frequent outpatient visits, and a variety of therapeutic approaches such as Cognitive Behavioral Therapy (CBT), Dialectical Behavior Therapy (DBT) and many more. I integrated prayer, journaling, and an array of self-care techniques into my daily routine.

The path to healing has been challenging and sometimes seemingly unending. Despite the countless hours dedicated to therapy and self-improvement, I've come to understand that the past never truly fades away; rather, I've learned to accept it, draw lessons from it, and use these insights to aid others. Healing from trauma is not a destination but a continuous, day-by-day process of personal growth and acceptance. Each step forward on this journey reinforces my resilience and reaffirms my commitment to becoming healthier and more self-aware.

"When you're born in a burning house,
you think the whole world is on fire. But it's not."
— **Richard Kadrey**

PART 3
MUSICAL HOMES

CHAPTER 11

BREAKING THE SILENCE

AS A CHILD, I had a knack for spinning tales, as many children do. Most of my lies were harmless, the kind they used to call little white lies back in the day. "Yes, I cleaned up my toys," I'd say, after shoving them all under the bed. "No Mama, I didn't push my brother, he tripped and fell into the wall," I'd insist with wide-eyed innocence. That said, my favorite lie, the one that landed me in serious trouble, was a prank gone terribly wrong.

My day took an unexpected turn after a normal dinner visit to my maternal Grandfather Clarence and Step Grandmother Denise's home, when I tried to play a prank on Mama. Instead of getting into our family's Root beer Brown Astro van, I crouched down on the back bumper with my fingers gripping tightly onto the open window frame. Excited, I waited patiently for Mama to back out of the driveway, looking forward to our freeway ride. I envisioned a wild adventure, with the wind in my hair.

Hidden from view, I shouted, "I'm back here!" to my mother as she entered the van. "I'm back here," I repeated, certain she would assume I was lying in the very back, behind the seat, where I had ridden many times before.

She started the van, backed out of the driveway, and drove down the road, completely unaware of my precarious position.

I succeeded! My accomplishment filled me with excitement. The adrenaline coursed through my veins, making me giddy, followed by an unnerving concern. I never considered how long the freeway ride would take or if I could hold on that long. Consumed by my short-term victory, I clung to the bumper of the van, feeling adventurous and terrified at the same time.

Suddenly, an ear-piercing whistle ripped through the air, interrupting my triumphant moment. My grandfather's earth-shattering whistle was a sound I knew all too well, and it stopped Mama in her tracks. The familiar, sharp tone jolted her, and she slammed on the brakes. She quickly jumped out of the van, her face a mix of confusion and concern, as she saw my grandfather yelling and waving his hands frantically from the top of the driveway. Although she was too far away to hear his exact words, my mother grasped that it had something to do with the back of the van. She hurried to the rear and found me there, frozen and clinging to the bumper. My fingers latched onto the window frame for dear life.

"What in the hell were you thinking, Tina!" she shouted, her voice a mix of shock and anger.

Her eyes were wide with disbelief as she stared at me, trying to comprehend what just happened.

"I, I, I was going to surprise you at the stop sign," I stammered, my voice small and trembling, trying to sound innocent.

Knowing damn well I was lying. I had every intention of riding this prank out to the end, but now, caught red-handed, I could only hope my shaky excuse would hold up.

The exhilaration of the prank had vanished, replaced by a sinking feeling of regret and fear. My reckless streak had gotten me into serious trouble this time, and the worry carved into Mama's face made it clear, I had pushed too far. Mama, still in shock, took a deep breath and helped me down from the bumper.

"Do you have any idea how dangerous that was?" she asked, her voice softer but still filled with concern. "You could have been seriously hurt."

I nodded, desperately trying to hold back the tears as the reality of what I had done hit me. A stark realization of the consequences had replaced the thrill of the prank.

My grandfather rushed toward us, his face a mix of stern disapproval and undeniable relief. His usual steady demeanor wavered slightly as he reached for me, pulling me into his arms. His embrace was firm yet warm, a silent reassurance that, despite everything, I was still safe, still his granddaughter.

With a voice that carried both love and authority, he gently but firmly warned, "You're lucky we caught you in time. You need to think before you act, Christina."

His words weren't just scolding; they were a plea, a reminder that my reckless choices had consequences. I could hear the worry beneath his tone, the unspoken fear of what could have happened if they hadn't stopped me. I nodded against his chest, swallowing the lump in my throat, knowing full well I had scared him just as much as I had scared myself.

On the drive home, Mama's expression, a mixture of anger and relief, was clear in her glances at me through the rearview mirror. A familiar silence hung in the air during the ride, a silence born of what had transpired.

The forty-five-minute drive home began with a stern, "Wait until your father hears about this. You are in deep shit."

Despite being busted, a quiet pride lingered for having the courage to do it. In all my eight years, this had to be my most adventurous lie, one that could have resulted in more than just a beating from Daddy. I learned a hard lesson that day, one that would stay with me for a long time. Little did I know my next lie would be the most devastating one of all.

Jennifer and Carrie Sullivan were sisters who rode the same bus as me to Pleasant Grove Elementary in Elk Grove, the last city we would call home as the Blackwell family. Though, in truth, my last name wasn't Blackwell. It was Brooks. My last name, though seemingly insignificant, always made me question my real father's identity. The Sullivan sisters were older girls who claimed their spots in the back of the bus, surrounded by the other sixth-grade children, where laughter, whispered secrets, and the occasional mischief thrived. I was the last pickup before heading to school, which meant only seats in the back were available. The sisters were pretty, vibrant, and confident, with many friends on the bus, unlike me. I sat quietly, listening to their conversations, desperately wishing I had something of value to add.

There came a day when I overheard the sisters chatting about bulls and cows. This was my chance, my opportunity to share some of my first-hand experience running from the bull that lived in the pasture down the road from our eight-acre home. I spent a lot of time outside, climbing into the neighbor's pasture and taunting the cows, donkeys, and the giant bull. I later found out his name was Max, short for

Maximus, as the owner shared with me the last time he caught me on his property.

Eager to join the conversation, I interrupted the girls, blurting out that one day I was wearing a red sweater and Max chased me to the fence. With a smirk, Jennifer, the ringleader of the crew, wasted no time correcting me.

"It had nothing to do with wearing red," her tone laced with amusement. "Bulls are colorblind." Just like that, she shut me down.

"Well, something got his attention because he chased me, and I barely got away!" I insisted, my cheeks flush with embarrassment.

The girls exchanged annoyed glances, and I retreated to my seat, quietly praying the bus would hurry and arrive at school. I wanted to be anywhere but there, away from the back of the bus and their dismissive laughter.

Following that, I remained quiet and avoided interrupting their conversations. I sat quietly, hanging onto their every word, hoping that just by listening; I might somehow absorb even a fraction of their effortless confidence. Mostly, I gazed out the window, mesmerized by the autumn masterpiece unfolding outside. The trees stood like living canvases, their branches adorned with breathtaking strokes of fiery reds, burned oranges, golden yellows, and deep earthy browns. Fall was in the air, and it has always been my favorite season. Our school was preparing for its annual Fall Festival that would take place that weekend, and I could not wait to attend. The anticipation of the festival gave me something to look forward to, a brief escape from the awkwardness of the bus ride.

One morning, my ears perked up as I overheard a boy casually ask Jennifer why she and Carrie lived with their grandparents instead of their parents. The question, seemingly simple, sent a jolt through me, igniting my undivided attention. I sat perfectly still, pretending to stare out the window, but every fiber of my being was tuned in, eager to catch her response. Jennifer, with no hesitation, explained that they live with their grandparents because their parents did bad things to them.

"Like what?" the little boy rudely belted, even though I was on the edge of my seat, desperate to know.

"They traded us for drugs. They would let people do bad stuff to us so they could get drugs."

"What kind of bad stuff?" the same boy blurted.

"Well, if you must know, they would do sex stuff to us. Now shut up," Jennifer replied.

That entire day in class, Jennifer's words echoed in my mind. I was so consumed by my thoughts that I got in trouble for not paying attention, which wasn't unusual for me. I often drifted away, losing myself in the maze of my own thoughts, a habit that, at the time, felt like second nature but would later make perfect sense when I was diagnosed with Attention Deficit Hyperactivity Disorder (ADHD) in my thirties. Jennifer's story, though different, resonated with me. There was a strange similarity to this quiet burden I carried. Her openness made me feel a mix of fear and hope. I had so many questions for her and Carrie. Why do these kinds of things happen? Who helped them make it stop? How could I be brave like they were? I wanted to get back on the bus and tell my truth, hoping they might have the answers I needed. Somehow, I thought they could help me.

As I sat in class, Jennifer's unsettling revelation looped in my mind like a scene from a horror movie; the kind I had once begged my Grandpa Gio to let me watch, swearing I wouldn't get scared and insisting to him that Mama let me watch scary movies at home. I had lied. That movie haunted me ever since, much like Jennifer's words did now, lingering in the shadows of my thoughts, refusing to let go. She had spoken so casually about living with her grandparents because her parents had done bad things to her and her sister. The weight of those words clung to me, leaving me feeling adrift in a sea of confusion and fear. The usual classroom chatter and the bustling energy of my classmates felt distant, like a muffled soundtrack in the background of my troubled thoughts. I stared blankly at the chalkboard, the teacher's words becoming a meaningless drone as I grappled with the implications of Jennifer's story.

Just as I was sinking deeper into my thoughts, the loudspeaker crackled to life, bringing me back to the present.

"Mrs. Anderson, please send Christina to the office. She will be leaving for the day."

My heart sank with disappointment. I had hoped to find a moment to talk to Jennifer, to understand more about her situation. But now, I was being pulled away, leaving my questions unanswered and my curiosity unquenched.

In the car with my mother, the silence was thick and suffocating. The usually comforting hum of the engine now felt ominous, a backdrop to my inner turmoil. I wrestled with whether to share what I had heard with my mother. Did she know about Jennifer and Carrie's situation? If she did, what did that mean for us? Could my mother be aware of the things happening in our own home and yet feel powerless to stop them, just as she seemed unable to protect us from Daddy's physical abuse?

I glanced at my mother; her face a mask of concentration as she navigated the familiar route to the doctor's office. The urge to speak up battled with a deep-seated fear of what might happen if I did. Would she dismiss my concerns, or worse, would she become angry? The fear of Daddy's wrath, should he find out I had spoken about our buried truth, left me paralyzed with fear.

As the car rolled on, mile after mile, the unspoken tension between us grew thicker. Each passing mile seemed to deepen the chasm of unanswered questions and unasked fears. My routine doctor's appointment loomed ahead, a mundane errand in stark contrast to the emotional storm brewing within me. Jennifer's story had opened a door to a part of my mind I kept tightly shut, and now I couldn't ignore the shadows that lurked there. The fear of my family sharing similar hidden truths weighed me down. I began to see the complexity of hidden stories and the silent struggles that shape our lives. The unspoken words riddled with shame and fear became a part of my reality, weaving a complex web of uncertainty and dread.

The next morning, I raced to the bus stop at the end of our long dirt road, determined to reach Jennifer and share my secret. My heart pounded with a mix of fear and resolve. As the bus approached, my chest tightened, and I felt a wave of nausea.

My feet seemed glued to the ground, and the bus driver had to call out, "Are you coming?"

Shaken out of my hesitation, I quickly hopped on and made my way to the back seat, plopping down next to Jennifer. She gave me a curious look, and before she could say anything, I blurted, "I need your help!"

"With what? Are you trying to chase bulls again?" she snickered, her tone light but her eyes serious.

"No," I whispered, barely audible. "My daddy does bad things to me."

Jennifer's face grew solemn, and she slumped down in her seat, creating a private space for us to talk. As I explained the awful things Daddy did, she cut me off.

"You need to talk to my grandmother. When can you come over?"

"I don't know. I'll have to ask my mom," I replied, my voice trembling.

"See if you can come over tomorrow after school. Do you have a piece of paper? I'll write my phone number and address. You can ride the bus to my house, and my grandmother can drive you home."

That evening, I nervously approached Mama and asked if I could go to Jennifer and Carrie's house after school. To my immense relief, she agreed and called their grandmother to plan. The next day, I rode the bus home with the sisters and met Mrs. Rose Whitfield, their grandmother. She was a short, gray-haired lady with a slow walk and an even slower way of speaking.

"Hello, dear!" she greeted me with a warm grin.

In an uncertain tone, I whispered, "Hello, Mrs. Whitfield,"

With a warm smile she replied, "Oh honey, you can call me Mrs. Rose."

The girls grabbed a snack at the kitchen table while Mrs. Rose sat across from me on the living room sofa.

"Would you like to tell me what's going on, dear?"

I hesitated and then started sharing the terrible things Daddy did to me when Mama was away. In that moment, hope swelled inside me like a fragile balloon. I truly believed Mrs. Rose might be the one. Someone who could finally help me escape from Daddy and the awful things he did to me behind closed doors. The fear was still there, clawing at my chest, whispering that he might find out and hurt me or Mama before I had the chance to get away. Yet, something stronger swelled up from deep within me, a fierce determination that guided me. For the first time, my courage outshouted my fear. Mrs. Rose's expression remained calm, though her eyes showed deep empathy. She nodded, listening intently.

"Would you mind if my friend, Officer Hamilton, came to see you and talk with you?" she asked softly. "He can take you to a safe place where your daddy can't hurt you anymore."

"What about my mama, my brother, and my baby sister? Would I still get to see them?"

"Yes, of course, dear. You just won't have to see your daddy anymore."

"I don't have any of my clothes, and I wouldn't get to say goodbye to Mama," I said, as tears glistened my eyes.

"Well, tonight's the fall festival. How about you ask your mother if you can stay with us for the weekend? That way, you can go home, get your clothes, and give your mama a big hug," Mrs. Rose suggested kindly.

She drove me home, and I eagerly asked Mama if I could go to the fall festival and stay the weekend at Jennifer and Carrie's house. Naturally, she said yes. I thanked her and hugged her tightly, taking in one last inhale of her familiar scent. There was a sense of excitement about the evening festival. For a moment, I had convinced myself that I was going to the fall festival that night. It wasn't until we pulled up to Jennifer's house and I saw Officer Hamilton's squad car in the driveway that the reality of what was happening sank in. There would be no fall festival, no sleepover. I wouldn't have to endure Daddy's abuse anymore, but I also wouldn't see Mama for an unknown amount of time. A storm of emotions churned inside me, confusion, guilt, and an aching sense of relief. I had lied to Mama, a lie that slipped so easily from my lips, yet weighed heavy on my heart. I felt guilty for betraying her trust, but beneath that guilt was a fragile flicker of hope, that maybe, just maybe, I was finally stepping toward safety. Choosing to share the truth came at a cost, even if it meant breaking Mama's heart in the process.

Officer Hamilton placed my bags in the back seat and drove for what seemed like hours to northern Sacramento. As we pulled into the parking lot, the tan building emerged ahead, its dull exterior giving away nothing of its purpose. It looked like an ordinary office building, the kind you might pass by without a second thought. The sign outside, partially obscured by overgrown shrubs, read: Department of Health and Human Services. Not knowing what that meant, I later found out it was the Child Protective Services (CPS) office. I felt confused and tired, wondering why we were there instead of my grandparents' house like Jennifer and Carrie went.

Officer Hamilton parked the car and guided me inside. Fluorescent lights buzzed overhead, casting a harsh glow on the beige walls that were adorned with outdated posters promoting child safety and wellness. The air was stale, tinged with a faint smell of cleaning supplies that failed to mask the underlying musty scent. The waiting area was sparsely furnished, with worn-out chairs upholstered in drab brown fabric that had seen better days. A few toys were scattered in a corner, looking neglected and un-kept, much like the children who had undoubtedly played with them.

The receptionist, a tired-looking older woman with dark circles under her eyes, and frizzy untamed curly hair cut above her shoulders, glanced up as we entered. She gave a small nod to Officer Hamilton and handed him a clipboard with forms to complete. I was directed to sit in one of the uncomfortable chairs, my feet barely touching the floor as I swung them nervously. A short time later, I was taken to a back room that resembled a doctor's office with an examination table covered by a thin roll of white paper taking center stage, flanked by a small desk and a single metal chair next to the door. The room was chilly and the metal chair was even colder on the back of my exposed thighs. Mama told me to wear pants to the fall festival, but I insisted on wearing shorts. I should have listened.

My brief stay on the metal chair was quickly interrupted as nurses bustled in and out, asking questions, taking my temperature, and checking my blood pressure. They then asked me to undress completely, which felt strange and uncomfortable. A thin hospital gown draped loosely over my compact frame, as I sat on the examination table, exposing my back to the cold air.

Dr. Hyngh entered, her presence commanding attention. She was a beautiful Indian woman with long black hair and tiny white clogs on her feet. Her demeanor was kind, yet professional, as she introduced herself and began the examination. I was mesmerized by her tiny feet and the way they moved gracefully across the floor, providing a minor distraction from the invasive nature of the exam.

After what felt like an eternity, a social worker appeared. She introduced herself as Jessica Myers but told me I could call her Jessica. Her appearance was slightly disheveled, her enormous nose stressed by the thick, coke-bottle glasses she wore. Her short hair framed a face that tried to be reassuring but couldn't hide the signs of exhaustion. She spoke in a gentle, yet firm tone, trying to explain what was happening, but most of her words were lost on me. All I understood was that I needed to follow her and bring my bags.

Jessica led me down a narrow, poorly lit hallway, the walls lined with doors, some slightly ajar, revealing small, cluttered offices and rooms filled with more toys and paperwork. The entire place felt suffocating, as if the walls themselves were closing in with the weight of unspoken stories and hidden fears.

She told me I would go to a temporary home until the courts could figure everything out. My heart sank at her words. This wasn't the plan.

I was supposed to be going to my grandparents' house, where it was safe and familiar. We exited the building, the oppressive atmosphere lifting slightly as we stepped into the crisp evening air. I should have listened to Mama and worn pants. The cold air shivered up my exposed legs and chilled my body. Jessica took me to a gray sedan, and as I climbed into the back seat, I couldn't shake the feeling of confusion and fear. Each mile of the silent drive to the temporary home pulled me farther from my known life and deeper into uncertainty.

The night encased us as we arrived at a quaint home in the unfamiliar city of Foothill Farms. As we pulled into the driveway, a modest house stood quietly under the dim glow of the streetlights, offering a stark contrast to the dark sky. In the driveway stood an elderly woman with snow white hair, her frail frame slightly hunched over. Her giant glasses magnified her kind eyes, and her almost comically crooked smile radiated warmth and comfort. She looked much older than either of my grandmothers, but there was an air of familiarity about her that put me at ease in a way I hadn't felt in a long time.

I had never seen this lady before, but her presence felt reassuring in that moment of profound uncertainty. Her welcoming smile and the way she stood there, waiting for us, seemed to promise a haven amidst the chaos that had become my life. She walked toward the car slowly, her movements deliberate yet tender, as if she had all the time in the world just for me.

As I stepped out of the car, she extended her hand, her voice soft and soothing. "Hello, sweetheart. I'm Delores Bennett, but you can call me Grandma Dee."

Her words wrapped around me like a warm blanket on a frosty night. I took her hand, feeling its gentle strength, and for the first time in a long while, I felt a glimmer of hope. The path ahead was filled with uncertainty, shadows of the past lurking in every corner. While standing there with Grandma Dee's comforting presence, I dared to believe that maybe, just maybe, I could find the safety I so desperately needed.

Christina Duke

CHAPTER 12

GUARDIAN ANGEL

AS I STEPPED INSIDE the small living room, I noticed the various knick-knacks and family photos adorning the walls and shelves, each telling a story of love and memories. The smell of freshly baked cookies lingered in the air, a stark contrast to the cold, clinical environment I had just left behind at the CPS office. My heart was still heavy with uncertainty, but the cozy warmth of Grandma Dee's home offered a small respite from my anxieties.

Midway into the living room, I observed a woman standing by the doorway to the kitchen. She was tall and skinny, with smooth, long brown hair that cascaded down her back. Her thick glasses magnified her eyes, giving her an almost owl-like appearance. She had a childlike innocence about her, and she seemed to move with a slight, awkward gait.

"This is my daughter, Charlotte," Grandma Dee introduced with a smile. "Charlotte, this is Christina."

Charlotte's face lit up with a warm, welcoming smile as she took a few steps toward me. Her movements were uncoordinated, and her walk had a slight shuffle to it, but there was an unmistakable kindness in her eyes. She spoke slowly and deliberately, her words laced with a gentle, melodic quality that made her seem endearing.

"Hi, Tina," Charlotte said, her voice filled with genuine warmth and curiosity. "It's nice to meet you."

"It's Christina!" I immediately corrected, my tone sharp and insistent.

Mama was the only person who called me Tina, and it felt like another betrayal to let a stranger use that name. My heart pounded as I clung to the small piece of my identity, desperate to keep some semblance of control in this unfamiliar situation. Allowing Charlotte to call me Tina felt like losing another piece of myself, and I wasn't ready for that. Not now, not here. Charlotte, taken aback by my forceful correction, stared at me for a moment.

Breaking the tension with a partial smile, she replied gently, "Hello Christina."

"Hi, Charlotte," I replied, reverting to my shyness, feeling a mix of awkwardness and curiosity myself. Meeting someone with Down Syndrome for the first time left me unsure of myself and how to proceed.

"Do you like cookies?" she asked, her eyes twinkling with excitement. "Mama made persimmon cookies. They're my favorite!"

I couldn't help but smile back at her infectious enthusiasm, although I did not know what persimmons were.

Feeling a bit more at ease, I replied, "I love cookies." It was a cookie after all. It had to be delicious.

"Come on, let's go to the kitchen!" Taking my hand, she led me toward the delicious aroma of freshly baked cookies.

As we entered the kitchen, Charlotte became more animated. She pointed excitedly to the plate of cookies on the counter, her eyes wide with delight.

"Look, Tina, I mean Christina! Aren't they beautiful?"

"They look delicious," I agreed, feeling a sense of warmth and comfort in Charlotte's presence.

Despite her Down Syndrome, which I was unfamiliar with, Charlotte had an undeniable charm and a heart full of kindness that immediately made me feel welcome. I couldn't help but wonder if all people with Down Syndrome were this cheerful and kind.

Grandma Dee's voice interrupted from the living room. "Just one, Charlotte. It's getting late and will be time for bed soon."

Charlotte's hand hovered over the plate of cookies as it searched for the perfect one. She quickly grabbed the biggest cookie and handed it to me on a napkin. My first bite into the persimmon cookie was a unique and delightful experience, a warm embrace of fall flavors. The cookie was soft and chewy, with the rich taste of sweet persimmon pieces and a mix of cinnamon, nutmeg, and cloves. It was unlike anything I had ever tried before, and before I knew it, I had devoured the entire cookie.

Making my way back into the living room, I realized Jessica was no longer there. Panic set in, and my eyes darted around the room and up and down the hallway. I felt a surge of anxiety. Why would she leave without saying goodbye? Did this mean I was alone now? Grandma Dee noticed my anxious behavior and spoke softly, trying to reassure me.

"Jessica will be in touch, and you will see her again real soon. Don't worry, sweetheart."

Her words were comforting, but they did little to silence the confusion and fear bubbling inside me.

"Would you like to see your room?"

"Yes, please," I replied, still puzzled, and a bit hurt by Jessica's sudden departure. I couldn't understand why she would leave without a word. It felt like another abandonment.

Grandma Dee slowly rose from her tattered recliner, her movements slow and deliberate. I followed her cautiously down the hall, each step filled with uncertainty.

"This is it, sweetheart," she said, patting the antique brown dresser that had clearly seen better days. "You can use this dresser, but don't use the bottom drawer; it's broken."

I took in the small room with its twin beds and two small dressers. It was simple, but had a certain charm. I chose the bed with the purple crocheted handmade quilt. The quilt's intricate patterns and soft fabric reminded me of the crocheted blankets my Aunt Cynthia made for all the children in the family. Though Aunt Cynthia hadn't made this one, it offered a sense of familiarity and comfort. As I ran my fingers over the quilt, I felt a mix of emotions. The fear and confusion of being in a new place, the sadness of being separated from my family, and a glimmer of hope that maybe this place could become a new home.

Grandma Dee's home gradually began to feel like my home over the next year. Except for a few temporary foster children who came and went, it was mostly just me, Grandma Dee, and Charlotte. We settled into a comforting nightly routine of homework, dinner, and what had become my favorite TV shows: *Wheel of Fortune* and *Jeopardy*. I rarely got the answers right, but the thrill of trying was something I looked forward to each evening. Grandma Dee would confidently shout her answers at the TV, and I'd immediately echo them, pretending they were my own. When the correct letters or answers were revealed, I'd either cheer with excitement or throw my hands up in playful disappointment, mirroring Grandma Dee's reactions.

Despite the growing sense of stability, waves of homesickness would crash over me unexpectedly, often bringing tears to my eyes. At school or in my new home, I'd find myself longing for my family, even occasionally missing Daddy. Mostly, I ached for Mama, my brother, and my sister.

Jessica, my social worker, would regularly pick me up for supervised visits with Mama. Sometimes my siblings would join us. I looked forward to these visits, but a nagging worry always lingered. Was Mama angry with me for telling on Daddy? We never spoke about it, so I focused on savoring every moment we had together. Our visits were bittersweet. Seeing Mama brought immense joy, but leaving her after each visit felt like ripping open a barely healed wound. Still, the hope of being with her, even for a short while, kept me going, and the time spent with Grandma Dee and Charlotte slowly started to mend my broken spirit.

Within a few weeks of moving in with Grandma Dee, in the fall of 1991, my world expanded rapidly. She began taking me to meet with doctors, lawyers, and behavior specialists, each asking the same probing questions about Daddy and the horrible things he made me do. It was like reliving the nightmare over and over, and it left me feeling vulnerable. I felt like a broken record, but amidst these repetitive and often uncomfortable encounters, one stood out: my weekly visits to my therapist, Ms. Liana.

From the moment I walked into Ms. Liana's office, I felt a sense of relief. Her office was a haven where I could escape the brutal questioning and just be a kid. We played games that made me forget, even if only for a little while, the dark shadows that loomed over my childhood. Ms. Liana would ask me about Daddy, Mama, and my family, but she did it in a way that felt gentle and caring. She encouraged me to draw pictures, and when she hung my artwork on her wall alongside other children's prized creations, I felt a spark of pride and belonging. Ms. Liana, with her bright blond hair and blue eyes, had a smile that made her top lip almost disappear. It made her look funny and would in turn, make me laugh.

The best part of these visits was when they were over, because Grandma Dee would take my hand and walk me across the parking lot to the culinary school, renowned for its delicious treats. Each week, I'd pick the biggest apple fritter I could find, and we would sit at the small iron tables in the dining area, savoring our sweet indulgence. Those moments with her made the tough sessions with Ms. Liana more bearable and became a cherished part of my routine.

Just as I found some semblance of normalcy in this new way of life, everything changed again. Toward the end of one of our sessions, Ms. Liana reached behind her desk and pulled out a large decorative gift bag. Confusion mixed with excitement as she handed it to me, announcing she had a surprise. I tore through the tissue paper to find a bright pink, fluffy teddy bear adorned with a shiny pink bow. Hugging it tightly, I felt a wave of unease. Why was she giving me a teddy bear? It wasn't my birthday, and I had done nothing special.

I looked up at Ms. Liana, my confusion mirrored in her saddened expression. Before I could voice my confusion, she spoke, her tone somber.

"Christina, this is our last session together. I've accepted a new job in Southern California and will be moving."

The words hit me like a punch to the gut. My insides knotted up, and I set the teddy bear beside me, feeling betrayed and abandoned. Why was she leaving? I had trusted her and opened up to her. Who was I going to talk to now? Was my therapy over? Would I still get apple fritters with Grandma Dee?

Silence filled the room as my mind raced with a thousand thoughts. Ms. Liana broke the silence, asking me to share what I was feeling.

"What did I do wrong? Why are you leaving me? I thought we were friends," my voice trembling as the tears grew heavy.

"Christina, look at me," Ms. Liana mumbled. "You did nothing wrong. This is not your fault, and you have been making significant progress. You'll still come here every week, but you'll see a new therapist named Jane Chadwick. She's a friend of mine and is excited to meet you and continue our work."

"I don't want to see her. I want you," I mumbled through the tears and snot that now streamed freely down my face.

Ms. Liana moved closer, wrapping her arm around me. "I know, sweetie. I want you to hug your teddy bear anytime you feel sad or think of me."

As I melted into her embrace, inhaling her sweet perfume, I tried to memorize the comfort of her touch as I sobbed uncontrollably.

The following week, I reluctantly returned to the building across from the culinary arts school. Ms. Jane took me to her office on the third floor. The brief thrill of riding the elevator quickly vanished as we stepped into her cold, unfriendly office. It was stark and uninviting, with no cozy couch or soft pillows, no children's artwork on the walls, and a peculiar smell that made me uneasy. Ms. Jane was nothing like Ms. Liana. Despite her best efforts, I could never build the same trust with her or feel comfortable enough to open up. The weekly sessions became a dreaded chore. The only solace I found was in the continued tradition with Grandma Dee, who never failed to take me for an apple fritter after each session. Those moments of sweetness became a minor comfort amid my growing disdain and reluctance to engage with my new therapist.

Each week, as I sat in Ms. Jane's office, I longed for the warmth and safety of Ms. Liana's presence. The transition was harder than I could have imagined, and the sense of betrayal and abandonment lingered. Ms. Jane's office, with its frigid atmosphere, felt empty compared to the comfort I had known with Ms. Liana. I couldn't help but feel a deep sense of loss, as if a part of my support system had been ripped away without warning.

Decades later, I would come to understand that this experience of abandonment set a tone for my future interactions with therapy. The pain and confusion of losing a trusted confidant made it extremely difficult for me to be receptive to new therapists. Each unfamiliar face was met with an inner wall of skepticism and guardedness, a protective mechanism born out of the fear of being hurt and abandoned again. The emotional scars from that time created a barrier, making it challenging to form the deep, trusting relationships necessary for effective therapy.

Looking back, those early experiences were more than just painful memories. They were pivotal moments that shaped the very foundation of how I viewed the world and the people in it. Losing faith and trust in those who were supposed to protect and nurture me created deep emotional fractures that took years to even begin to understand. Every broken promise, every instance of betrayal, reinforced the belief that I wasn't safe, that people couldn't be trusted, and that love often came with conditions or consequences.

This mistrust didn't just affect my relationships, it seeped into every corner of my life. It showed up in my friendships, my romantic partnerships, and most notably, in my difficulty forming bonds with therapists and other helping professionals. I craved support, yet feared it at the same time. I often sabotaged connections or pulled away before anyone could disappoint me. The idea of vulnerability felt dangerous, and being truly seen felt like a risk I couldn't afford to take.

Those early ruptures taught me how essential stability and trust are in the therapeutic relationship. Without them, healing feels impossible. It wasn't until I encountered individuals who showed consistency, patience, and compassion, who didn't flinch at my walls or run when things got hard, that I softened. And in that softening, I found the beginnings of true healing.

Recognizing the impact of those early betrayals has been one of the most vital steps in my journey toward self-acceptance. It has helped me untangle the false narratives I clung to for so long that I was unworthy of love or destined to be alone. These realizations haven't erased the pain, but they've helped me make peace with it. They've reminded me of the incredible resilience I've built, not in spite of my wounds, but because of them.

CHAPTER 13

ROOTS REVEALED

I'LL NEVER FORGET THE evening we gathered around the kitchen table, savoring our weekly dinner of Hamburger Helper, buttered sliced bread, and canned green beans, as Grandma Dee unexpectedly reached across the table and clasped my hand. Her touch was gentle, but her eyes carried a seriousness that made my gut twist with unease. I put down my fork, my appetite vanishing.

"What's wrong?" I asked, my voice edged with worry.

"Nothing's wrong sweetheart, but I have something to tell you and don't want you to get upset."

I waited with anticipation as she explained I had an appointment to meet with a new therapist, but for about two or three sessions only. Confusion clouded my thoughts.

"Do I still have to see Ms. Jane?" I asked, my tone hopeful, silently praying she'd say no. I couldn't stand those endless prying sessions with Ms. Jane.

"Yes," Grandma Dee confirmed, crushing my hopes. "You'll still be seeing Ms. Jane, but this new therapist is going to talk to you about some other things."

"What things?" I pressed, trying to make sense of it all.

"I'm not sure, honey," she admitted, her thumb gently stroking my knuckles, "but I'll be there with you the whole time, I promise."

The comfort of her words, especially her solemn promise, calmed me a little. When Grandma Dee promised something, she meant it. That simple assurance held a weight that always made me feel safer.

The next day, she picked me up from school early. I was disappointed because I'd been chosen for an exclusive after-school art program, with only twenty students school-wide receiving invitations. Mr. O'Connor, my teacher, had praised my art skills, telling me I had great potential. Missing that first class felt like a punishment, and I couldn't help but feel resentful. I expected our usual long drive downtown to Ms. Jane's office, where the only highlight was the chance to get an apple fritter afterward. But this time, the drive was short. We pulled up to a place I didn't recognize, a house with a sign on the lawn covered in words I couldn't pronounce. The only one that made sense to me was the word therapy. I sighed. Great! No art class and no donuts.

Inside, the waiting room was unfamiliar, and I clung to Grandma Dee's side, feeling small and out of place. A woman walked out to greet us, and I immediately noticed how beautiful and exotic looking she was. Her hair was a short salt-and-pepper afro, and her skin glowed with confidence I envied. She wore large wooden earrings in the shape of Africa, and her colorful Dashiki caught my eye, so vibrant and full of life.

"Hi there," she said warmly, her laugh surprisingly deep and hearty for someone so petite. "I'm Ms. Yolanda Robertson."

I stared at her, mesmerized by her presence. She was captivating, and for a moment, I forgot where I was. Grandma Dee nudged me gently.

"Ms. Robertson is ready to see you," she said.

"Aren't you coming?" I asked in a shaky tone.

Grandma Dee gave me a reassuring smile. "I'll be right here when you come out. You'll be okay, I promise."

Her promise worked its magic again, wrapping me in a thin layer of courage.

I followed Ms. Robertson into her office, which was nothing like Ms. Jane's bleak, boring space. This room was bursting with color, artwork hanging on every wall, shelves overflowing with books, and board games stacked neatly in one corner. My nervousness gave way to curiosity. Maybe this wouldn't be so bad.

Ms. Robertson sat across from me, her eyes kind but focused.

"Christina," she began, "do you know why you're here?" I nodded, resigned. "To talk about the bad stuff Daddy did to me."

Her eyes softened with understanding. "I'm so sorry that happened to you. You didn't deserve that, and it wasn't your fault."

Her words settled over me like a gentle warmth, but then she shifted the conversation.

"I read in your file that you used to look through photo albums and ask your mom if the man in her school dance picture was your real dad. What made you think Curtis wasn't your father?"

"Because he was mean to me," I said simply. "He was nice to my brother and sister, but he always treated me different."

Ms. Robertson leaned in a little closer. "How would you feel if I told you that Curtis isn't your biological father?"

"My what?" Unsure of her unfamiliar term.

"Your real daddy," she clarified.

Relief washed over me. "Oh, I'd be glad," I said, almost laughing at the absurdity of it. "That's what I thought for a long time."

A smile tugged at her lips. "Well, you were right. Curtis is not your biological father. If you'd like, I can tell you about the man who is."

"Okay," I whispered, my mind spinning. A part of me felt vindicated, like a mystery I had always known existed was finally being solved.

Ms. Robertson pulled out a board game and set it up between us.

"I'd like to play a game with you, if that's alright."

My heart lifted a little, my eyes lit up in excitement, yet still processing the explosion that had just went off in my mind. Games were something I could handle. As she explained the rules, I found myself getting absorbed in the dice rolls and the colorful game board. It differed from any game I had played before; it was like Monopoly but was all about people from around the world. The cards asked questions about people and their cultures or shared facts about different nationalities. I drew a card that asked something on the lines of, "What do you know about African American people?"

Caught off guard and feeling uncertain about the right answer, I hesitated. "I don't know," I mumbled. "I mean, I like their hair."

Ms. Robertson laughed, a sound that filled the room with warmth. "What do you like about it?"

"It's really cool," I replied, feeling a little shy but glad she wasn't upset.

"Do you know any Black people?" she asked. I perked up, eager to get this question right.

"Yes! My friend at school, Kendra. She's Black, I mean African American."

Ms. Robertson's smile widened. "It's okay to say Black people. What if I told you that your real dad is Black? How would that make you feel?"

Confusion clouded my mind. I looked down at my pale arm, as if trying to find the connection.

"But... I don't look Black."

She nodded, her voice gentle. "Black people come in all different shades. Some are darker, like me," she said, holding out her hand, "and some are much lighter. Here, let me show you."

She pulled out pictures of light-skinned Black people, albino Black people, and those who looked almost Hispanic. I stared at the images, trying to reconcile this new information.

"Do you have a picture of my dad?" I finally asked, a flicker of hope in my voice.

She shook her head. "I don't, but I can tell you about him. His name is Darius, and he's very excited to meet you."

Two sessions later, Ms. Robertson said I was ready to meet my father, Darius Knight. The man who had unknowingly haunted my dreams, the father I had never known, was suddenly very real. I left her office that day carrying two undeniable truths: Curtis Blackwell was no longer the man I'd call Daddy, and my real father was out there, waiting to meet me. Where I would go from there, I wasn't sure. But I was ready to find out.

The day I met my biological father unfolded like a surreal scene from a movie, one that I had played over and over in my mind but could never quite predict. My social worker had arranged the meeting at McDonald's, likely hoping that the bright colors and the familiar smell of fries would soften the weight of this life-altering encounter. As we drove there, a whirlwind of curiosity, hope, and fear tumbled through me. My heart beat faster with every mile, and when we finally pulled into the parking lot, I gripped the car seat, bracing myself for whatever would come next.

Inside, the joyful commotion of children laughing and the cheerful décor clashed painfully with the anxiety coursing through me. The social worker led me to a table near the window, where a tall, light-skinned Black man stood. His mini afro framed his robust face, his broad shoulders tense with anticipation. His thin beard and mustache couldn't mask the nervousness in his eyes, eyes that searched mine as if trying to find a piece of himself reflected there. Beside him stood a petite white woman with soft curls and a warm, reassuring smile.

The social worker introduced them. "Christina, this is your father, Darius, and your stepmother, Priscilla."

Priscilla's presence radiated a calm that felt almost magical, momentarily soothing on my anxious nerves. I quickly returned my attention to Darius, my father, the man whose blood ran through my veins, yet who felt like a stranger. His unease only added to my own, and for a moment, I wondered if he was as terrified as me. We exchanged awkward greetings, our words heavy with the weight of everything unsaid. I sat across from him, feeling small and uncertain, picking at the Happy Meal my social worker had handed me. Darius forced a smile, but the discomfort was palpable. The air between us grew thick, broken only by the background noise of kids squealing and parents chatting.

Finally, in a desperate attempt to break the ice, Darius leaned forward.

"Do you want to go play in the playground?" he asked, his eyes lighting up with a glimmer of hope.

His suggestion surprised me, and for the first time that day, I felt a spark of excitement. I nodded, and we stood together, the tension easing slightly.

The McDonald's Play Place was a colorful maze of plastic tunnels, slides, and a ball pit that looked like a sea of rainbow gems. As we climbed through the winding tubes, something miraculous happened. The awkwardness between us melted away. We maneuvered through the narrow spaces, laughing as we bumped into each other. I couldn't help but giggle at the sight of him, a grown man, six feet three inches tall, awkwardly navigating the child-sized tunnels, his limbs barely fitting. In the ball pit, we tossed plastic balls at each other, and for those precious moments, the world felt light. We were just father and daughter, playing and laughing, as if we had known each other forever. The simple joy of that moment created a connection, a fragile but genuine bond for which I had been yearning. When we finally emerged, sweaty and out of breath, the heaviness that had clouded the start of the day had lifted, replaced by a cautious optimism. As we walked back to our table, I felt a bit of hope rise on the inside; a hint of excitement in getting to know my real father. The day had begun with tension and uncertainty but ended with a glimmer of something I desperately needed, the possibility of love and belonging. Meeting Darius was like finding a puzzle piece that had been missing from the picture of my life. It didn't complete the image, but it brought me a step closer.

In the following months, I began visiting Darius and Priscilla at their home in Oak Park, a small, unique town in Sacramento. I had been told that I had half-siblings, though I hadn't met them during the supervised visits. My first time at their house was an overwhelming whirlwind of sights, sounds, and emotions. The sudden, loud slam of the metal security door startled me as I crossed the threshold, leaving me puzzled and uneasy. Before I could calm my nerves, an overexcited, scruffy white poodle named Tuffy greeted me. The dog jumped on me, barking and licking with an enthusiasm to which I was unaccustomed. My only experience with dogs had been Grandpa Brooks' Beagle, Corky, who was old and dignified, spending most of his time napping on a plush cushion. Tuffy, with his dirty fur and boundless energy, felt like an invasion of my already frazzled personal space. Naturally, we did not hit it off.

Darius led me through the house, and I took in every detail like a detective gathering clues. The living room had dated wood paneling on the walls, and in the center hung a large piece of driftwood lacquered to a glossy finish, with a mirror embedded in the middle. The rest of the wall was a cluttered collage of photos, some carefully framed, and others haphazardly taped up to the wood paneling. My eyes scanned each image, desperate to recognize a face, to feel a sense of familiarity. All of them were strangers. My eyes moved into the adjoined dining room, and I found my favorite wall. It was an eclectic patchwork of corkboard squares and mirrors that reached from the floor to the ceiling. The arrangement fascinated me, and I wondered about the memories pinned there, about the reflections captured over the years.

A roar of laughter, yelling, and multiple loud conversations greeted me in the hall as my father led me to a room full of children, some younger than me, but most of them older. Two sets of bunk beds consumed the room with a dresser in the middle topped with a TV and video game system.

Upon entering, the room became silent and multiple sets of eyes focused on me as Darius introduced me to the group. When I say introduced, I mean he said, "this is Christina, introduce yourself and make her feel welcome."

He may as well have thrown me into a pack of wolves. Lewis and Alexander, my half-brothers, along with Dominique, my half-sister, and their friends and cousins, introduced themselves almost simultaneously, briefly interrupting their video games before resuming them. I stood in the doorway for a moment until Lewis motioned for me to sit down. I looked around for an empty spot, but two people occupied each bed and others had taken the middle chairs.

He casually exclaimed, "Get in where you fit in!" a phrase that would become all too familiar.

Nervously, I sat on the edge of one of the bunk beds. The noise level was triggering for me. I felt myself flinching at each outburst of laughter, at every sudden movement. Loud noises had always been a source of anxiety, a stark reminder of yelling, of arguments that could shift into something worse in an instant. They hurled playful insults that I couldn't quite process, and I interpreted them as mean and hurtful, but they just laughed, as though being called names was a game. I didn't know how to handle it. My feelings were hurt more times than I cared to admit, much so that I developed a knot of defensiveness in my chest. Over time, I grew thicker skin, learning to roll with the teasing. It was a different survival, one that required humor and resilience.

In this hectic new environment, Priscilla became my lifeline. Small and sweet, with a gentle voice that could soothe even the most restless spirit, she had a way of bringing calm to the storm. Priscilla's presence was warm and protective, a balm for my frayed nerves. As soft-spoken as she was, I soon learned she had an angry side, which was rarely seen, but when it reared, it was like watching a tidal wave rise, a force with which one did not care to reckon. Luckily, she only unleashed that fierceness when necessary, and she never directed it at me. For me, she remained a source of comfort.

The honeymoon phase of finally having a father wore off faster than I had expected during these biweekly visits. The resentment I carried for all the years of suffering, for the childhood stolen from me, bubbled to the surface. I blamed him openly for his absence, for not being around to protect me from the horrors I'd endured. Priscilla often found herself in the middle of these confrontations, acting as a mediator between my anger and my father's defensiveness. She had a way of calming me down, taking me aside and offering quiet reassurances.

Our fight for justice loomed over everything. Priscilla stood by me, even when it meant sitting in stark courtrooms as I relived my trauma repeatedly. We went to court three times while I was in foster care. Lawyers asked me to describe every painful detail, followed by drawing pictures of body parts I should have never been exposed to. At ten-years old, I was grilled by defense attorneys trained to confuse and disorient, causing me to sound like an unreliable witness. Never fully understanding why I had to keep repeating this public process made it feel like a punishment.

In the back of the courtroom, I could see my Grandpa Clarence and Step Grandmother Denise and my Grandmother Marilyn and Step Grandfather Gio. Collectively, they were always just Grandma and

Grandpa to me, no step attached. The reunion was fleeting, a slight moment of connection in a sea of bureaucracy and heartbreak. I clung to it, even though it brought no real resolution, and I was not permitted to speak to or hug them.

In the end, all the reliving, all the retelling, the painful act of tearing open wounds I had barely begun to heal led to nothing. The charges were dropped and Curtis walked away, a free man.

"Because he didn't break the hymen, there wasn't enough evidence to put him in jail," Jessica explained the last time I had to visit the courtroom.

That phrase would echo in my mind for years, sounding clinical and absurd, as though my pain had been reduced to a sterile, cold technicality. My innocence, my childhood, had been stolen from me, but the system labeled my abuser a gentleman, as if his crimes could be sanitized and excused because he hadn't left the right kind of scars.

It was a lesson that burned itself into my mind, searing through every hope I had clung to. Justice was a mirage, a shimmering facade that existed only to relieve the guilty of their sins. It did not exist to protect or vindicate the innocent. The courtroom, with its stern judges and indifferent lawyers, felt like a cruel theater where my suffering had been put on display, only to be dismissed when the final curtain fell.

Left holding pieces of shattered hope, I grappled with the reality that the world I lived in was far from fair. The betrayal of the justice system cut deeper than any wound Curtis had inflicted. It told me, loud and clear, that my pain wasn't significant enough, that the destruction of my body and spirit didn't warrant retribution. The little girl who had screamed for help, who had begged the world to see her, now learned that no one truly cared. From the adults who were supposed to protect me, to the legal system I was taught to believe in, they had all let me down.

The verdict didn't just break my heart; it shattered the fragile sense of safety I had been trying to rebuild. It made me question everything: my worth, my place in the world, the very concept of right and wrong. I wondered if I would ever feel safe, if I could ever trust anyone to stand up for me or believe me. The court's dismissal of my trauma left a gaping wound, a void filled with doubt, anger, and an overwhelming sense of unimportance.

The emotional damage seeped into every part of my being, poisoning the way I saw myself and the world around me. I internalized the lie that my pain didn't matter and that I wasn't worth defending. It planted seeds of shame that tangled their roots deep into my psyche, whispering that I was broken, unworthy, and unlovable. I walked out of that courtroom feeling smaller than ever, like a ghost of the girl I used to be, destined to haunt my own memories.

As I grew older, the verdict followed me like a shadow. It made trust feel impossible, turned relationships into battlegrounds, and left me constantly searching for validation, approval, and a sense of belonging I feared I would never find. Justice had failed me, but the damage left in its wake lived on, an echo that would take years of healing and self-discovery to even begin to quiet. And yet, through the darkness, a small ember of defiance burned inside me. Somehow, despite the crushing weight of betrayal, I vowed I would one day reclaim my story, even if the world had chosen not to hear it.

CHAPTER 14

THROWN INTO CHAOS

ACTIONS HAVE CONSEQUENCES. I used to think that was just something adults said to scare kids into behaving, but the day I got into a fight with Kendra Carter, I learned just how true those words could be. We started out as friends; she was the only friend I made at Pioneer Elementary, the new school I started since moving into foster care with Grandma Dee. For months, Kendra and I sat together in class and dominated the playground in the popular 90s elementary school game of "Red Rover," a game now banned in school across America because of its propensity for causing injuries. We saw it as weeding out the weak, but in reality, it was a way for children to clothesline other children in the name of fun. On one side of the field, children would line up next to each other and hold hands to make an indestructible wall. On the opposite side of the field, children would run at full speed, embracing their inner cheetah, hoping to separate the hands of two children, resulting in them breaking through. Strength and speed could get you through, crowning you champion. Sadly, for most children, it resulted in being hit in the neck or chest by a set of arms, usually knocking the wind out of the runner and causing them to plummet to the ground, marking them as weak and losers. Kendra and I, however, were a powerhouse. We were unstoppable and ran through those kids like linebackers playing in the super bowl.

In class that morning, I had some exciting news to share with Kendra. Recently learning about my father's African American heritage left me excited and hopeful about the new connections I would have in the Black community. For the first time, I felt a sense of belonging. Since my father was Black, I now considered myself part of the Black community, and I hoped Black children would befriend me because of our shared heritage. How naive and desperate I was! I leaned over to Kendra during our morning instruction and shared my newfound news with her.

"Hey guess what!"

"What" she whispered with a look of curiosity.

"My real dad is Black. I'm Black just like you, well partially Black, I guess."

"Um, no, you are not Black," she laughed, dismissing my excitement.

"I am, only my dad's not dark Black, he's light Black."

"You mean he's albino?"

"No, not albino, just lighter than you are; look, let me show you. Hold out your palm." Reluctantly, she held out her palm, which was much lighter than the rest of her body. "He's light like that," I said with a sense of pride and excitement.

Unable to finish the conversation, our teacher, Mr. O'Connor, put our names on the board for talking. Getting your name on the board was strike one and two tick marks next to it meant we would lose recess or after school detention.

Excited to continue our conversation during recess, I tried to continue to convince Kendra that my dad was Black and therefore I was Black, or mixed, as the therapist taught me.

"Hey everybody, Christina says her dad is Black, and she thinks she's Black now."

Kendra shared with the crowd of children jokingly. An eruption of laughter rang out in disbelief, and it became the running joke of recess amongst the playgrounds. My friend's disbelief offended and hurt me because I didn't understand why it was funny. I retreated to the bench, anxiously awaiting the bell ending recess. After the recess bell, we lined up in our usual spots and Kendra was still on full display with her comedy bit. We argued in line and she called me a "wanna be." She said I didn't even know who my real father was and if I thought it was a Black man, I was stupid.

Her words cut; aimed at that raw, sore place I kept hidden behind my bravado. Before I realized what I was doing, I lunged at her, my fists flying, rage spilling out in a flurry of swinging arms and tangled hair. Our fight lasted less than thirty seconds but was enough to wound our friendship and entertain the multiple classes of bystanders. "Fight, fight, fight!" The students chanted, drawing the attention of our six-foot, red-haired, freckled faced teacher who seamlessly ripped us apart in one swoop, controlling us by using one arm each. His grip was firm, but not unkind. His stern voice immediately calmed us and sent us to the principal's office for our inevitable suspension. Before Grandma Dee arrived to pick me up, Kendra and I met with the school counselor and made up and were back to laughing and joking. I knew I would be in trouble when I got home, but I didn't realize yet that this fight would set off a chain of events I could never undo.

That weekend, I was supposed to go to the zoo with my social worker, but Grandma Dee, the closest thing I had to stability, put her foot down.

"You will not be going to the zoo this weekend," she stated matter-of-factly.

For the first time, I completely understood that the consequence of my action was appropriate. My punishment fit the crime; I understood and accepted this with unexpected maturity, though I was disappointed about missing the zoo. When she shared the news with my social worker upon her arrival to pick me up, things became heated between the two. My social worker bristled, pride coloring her voice as she argued back. She didn't like being challenged, especially not by a foster guardian.

"I have the authority here," she snapped, her eyes narrowing. "You can't make that decision."

"If I'm responsible for disciplining her, then I decide, and she isn't going." Grandma Dee's voice remained firm with steel beneath her words.

I understood I'd messed up, and I was okay with the punishment. However, my social worker's wounded pride and disdain for being challenged would change my life forever. By Sunday evening, I had to pack my meager belongings into white plastic trash bags, ready to be shuffled into a new foster home. I couldn't make sense of why I had to leave. The confusion tangled with a crushing guilt that pressed down on my chest, heavy and unrelenting. My heart ached as I left Grandma Dee's house, the only place that had ever felt like an actual home.

Despite my social worker's many attempts to explain her decision and coax me into conversation, I remained silent, my eyes fixed on the blurred scenery outside the car window. Tears spilled down my cheeks in steady streams, my small body trembling as I tried to contain the sobs threatening to escape. The weight of yet another uprooting crushed my chest, making it hard to breathe, hard to think, hard to do anything but grieve in silence. The world outside rushed past in streaks of gray and muted browns. I stared off aimlessly, paying little attention to my surroundings. I was looking at everything I was leaving behind. Every turn of the car felt like a painful yank, pulling me farther from whatever scraps of stability to which I had clung. My social worker spoke gently, her voice a mix of firmness and forced optimism. Her words felt like static, meaningless noise drowning in the sea of my sorrow. I wanted to believe her reassurances that this move would be different, that this home would be better. Hope felt dangerous, a cruel trick I had fallen for too many times before. So I just sat there, my head pressed against the cool window, the city I once called home fading behind me as we made our way toward yet another unfamiliar house, yet another set of strangers, yet another attempt at belonging. And all because of my choice to have a stupid thirty-second fight with Kendra. How could I have been so foolish? My thoughts spiraled, each one hitting harder than the last. This was all my fault. The shame gnawed at me from the inside out, and I couldn't stop mentally tearing myself apart.

Caroline and Bernard Sinclair's house was nothing like Grandma Dee's. For starters, there were other kids, some older, some younger. The house was uninviting, and my new foster mother smoked and the house had a wretched odor to it. Caroline and Bernard were efficient, detached, and strangely focused on saving resources in ways that felt dehumanizing.

"We shower together here," Caroline announced on my first night. "To save water."

I stared at her, horrified, hoping it was a poor joke. The thought of standing under the shower with strangers, bare and vulnerable, made my skin crawl. In a place where rules were rules, my comfort didn't matter. My new foster parents cooked meals that were foreign to me, spicy stews and pungent curries that made my eyes water. The house felt foreign and unwelcoming, a far cry from Grandma Dee's warm kitchen, and there were no warm persimmon cookies to welcome me. In fact, they didn't allow us to have sweets, so dessert was a thing of the past.

I looked forward to the promise from my social worker that I would still have my own room, a luxury I relished at Grandma Dee's and with which I had become quite comfortable. That, however, was an empty promise. The teenager who occupied the room with me was obnoxiously loud and wreaked of body odor. My only respite was when she left every weekend, a process reserved for foster children preparing to move back home. I was left to entertain myself and bound to my bedroom or the driveway as my play area. While the children ate in the dining area, my foster parents dined separately in their living room, an off-limits area for children.

Grandma Dee spared no expense in buying me nice clothes. My wardrobe was small, but I had well-made clothes, and, better yet, they were all mine. Over the first few weeks, at Caroline and Bernard's, my clothes started disappearing. I informed Caroline and was met with little concern, other than her informing me I better keep up with my clothes because she would not be buying me new ones any time soon. Week after week, I complained about the disappearance of my items until one Friday evening Caroline came bursting into my room right before my roommate was to leave for good and be reunited with her mother. Caroline took the girl's duffel bag that was sitting near the door next to the paper bag full of her shoes and ripped each item out while tossing it on her bed. Unsure of what was happening, I retreated to the corner of my bed that was far away from whatever this was that was going on until I recognized some items being thrown on the bed.

"Those are my shorts, that's my shirt, those are my panties," I cried out.

The girl stood frozen by the door. Caroline told me to find what was mine and put it in my drawer and stormed out of the room. Not a single word passed between us, the silence thick with unspoken tension.

Thankfully, within an hour or two, her mother arrived, gathered her things, and just like that, she was gone for good.

My heart ached, waiting for Caroline to believe me, to acknowledge that I had been telling the truth all along. I longed for her to offer some reassurance, to say she understood, to make it right by replacing the clothes that had disappeared weekend after weekend at the hands of my thieving roommate. That moment never came. No validation, no apology, and no new clothes. The entire ordeal was swept under the rug, as if it never happened, and just like that, I learned another hard truth: sometimes the people you expect to make things right simply don't. I played in the driveway for a few more weeks until my social worker unexpectedly moved me overnight to my third foster home, after only six weeks with the Sinclair's.

With no explanation, no warmth, not even a trace of empathy, my social worker delivered the news with a practiced flatness: "Your new home will be a better place for you." A phrase I had heard before. It was the same line I'd been fed after my last move. A phrase that, in fact, had lost any meaning. I knew better now. "Better" didn't exist. Her words didn't bring comfort. They only carved a deeper hollow inside me. This wasn't a transition, it was another abandonment. All I could do was brace myself for whatever "better" meant this time.

The drive to my next foster home was much shorter than the previous two. My new foster parents, Josephine and Elliot Winslow, were good friends with Caroline and Bernard, and lived about fifteen minutes down the road. Their home was much larger, a lot nicer, and bursting at the seams with teenagers. A motley crew of foster children who had formed their own survival club greeted me in the traditional teenager way...by ignoring me and acting as if I did not exist. I was too young to be of any interest or use to the group of female foster teens on the verge of aging out of the system. At ten years old, I was the youngest, and this new environment was wild, lawless, and full of sarcastic foul-mouthed teenagers. Intrigue and fear consumed me simultaneously. Josephine and Elliot were not strict and allowed their foster children to come and go as they pleased, which included me as well.

Josephine was an average sized woman with beautiful olive skin, gentle features and long black and silver kissed hair. She smoked as well. Sometimes a couple of the older teens would smoke with her as they shared the latest gossip from the fast-food restaurants where they worked. Josephine was more of a friend to the teens than an authority figure. Elliot, on the other hand, was freakishly tall with an intimidating rough voice and had a propensity for yelling to get his point across. He proudly sported a beer keg for a belly that prevented him from leaning over and putting on his own socks. That responsibility always fell on the youngest foster child; a burden passed down like an unspoken rule, and now that unfortunate child was me. Helping Elliot put on his socks made me nauseous and caused me to wash my hands with extra soap each time. His toenails were long and jagged and stained with a yellowish tint that looked like something rotten. The pungent smell caused me to hold my breath as I struggled to force the unforgiving tube socks over his size 14 creature-like feet.

Not everything about Elliot was awful. He was a professional billiard player with a giant pool table in the main living room. My interest in the sport inspired him to teach me how to play. This mostly comprised him showing off all the amazing combination shots while listening to him boast about his advanced skill that made him better than every other professional out there. Weekends frequently involved watching VHS tapes of billiard competitions. Each watch party started out with my retrieval of three cans of grape Shasta soda and a family size bag of cheddar and sour cream Ruffles chips. I could usually sneak out of the room after consuming a handful of chips and finishing my grape soda, leaving Elliot left to destroy the remaining bag of chips and the other sodas.

Of the three foster homes I had experienced, Josephine and Elliot by far had the largest backyard, equipped with a metal swing set that stood defiantly in the yard's corner, a relic from a time when safety was a mere afterthought, and childhood bruises and scars were badges of honor. Chains dangled from the top bar, their once shiny silver links now dulled and corroded in rust, clinking in the breeze like some forgotten wind chime of childhood adventures. The kind of chains that bit into small palms and left angry red marks as they twisted and pulled under the weight of a swinging child. The seats of the swings, flat and unforgiving slabs of hard plastic, seemed to beckon with a quiet menace, promising equal parts thrill and pain to those who dared to ride. With a house full of teenagers too cool to be bothered with a swing set, let alone the backyard, I was delighted to have this mischief magnet all to myself.

Adopting my older foster sister's provocative sense of style while now sporting tiny tank tops bearing my midriff accompanied by frayed booty shorts, I allowed my exposed skin to become beautifully Sun-kissed after the painful sunburn resided. Sunscreen was no longer a requirement for hot summer days as it had been when living with Mama. Josephine would simply hand me a bottle of green aloe gel to lather on my burns in the evenings when she got tired of hearing me complain. The sun's aftermath was not enough to deter me from turning their backyard into my imagination's destination. Causing the legs of the swing set to teeter off the ground while thrusting my 100-pound body forward as high as I could became a daily challenge. When the dopamine wore off and the dangerous thrill no longer excited me, I would venture into the next adrenaline rush. After climbing to the top of the "A" frame structure, with my arms stretched out, I would take turns balancing on one foot like a trained gymnast, willing myself to attempt a handstand like I had seen on TV, but talking myself out of the idea every time. If only I had more courage, I thought.

My stay with Josephine and Elliot coincided with the summer Olympics held in Barcelona, Spain that year. Inspired by the gymnast's well-choreographed, effortlessly presented floor routines, I created my unique routine, using the front yard's perfectly square grass area as my Olympic floor. I practiced my impressive and elegant routine, showcasing a combination of grace, strength, and precision. When I was ready to showcase my talents, I eagerly and anxiously summoned all my foster home's residents as an audience. One of the nine current occupants granted me an audience. Well, two if you count the dog. Elliot, holding his mangy poodle, his prize possession second to his pool table, stood in the doorway offering his esteemed words of encouragement of, "Get it over with."

I ran to the corner, took a breath and began my routine, a series of partially lifted cartwheels, sloppy somersaults and flailing arms, that in my mind, were enough to earn me the gold medal and a spot on the podium, replacing that year's current winner. Upon completing my prize routine, I landed in my rehearsed spot facing the front of the house with my arms in superstar mode, proudly above my head. My exaggerated grin bearing all my teeth quickly turned into a sad, tight-lipped frown as I witnessed the closed brown door of the house where Elliot once stood. The tiny marble of trust Elliot had built with me over the last few weeks shattered in that moment. The category of distrusting men that included my stepfather and biological father was now shared by my foster father.

Although Elliot tried to continue his routine of spending time with me, I was no longer interested and made sure he knew it. My once playful, childlike personality took a dark turn. Afternoons of playing in the yard turned into desperate attempts to connect with my teenage foster sisters. Using the weekly allowance the Winslow's provided, I paraded the downtown streets of West Sacramento checking out the local stores, buying outfits that were inappropriate for my age, and splurging on makeup that was the wrong color for anyone not wearing a Halloween costume. My new passion became dressing like the other teens, and the girls, seeing my efforts to mature quickly, motivated me to learn how to apply makeup and tease my bangs correctly, creating inches of volume and drenching them in a full can of Aqua Net hair spray. Not only did I begin to dress and act like them, I picked up on the sassy, disrespectful comebacks they often barked at Elliot during daily screaming matches.

Despite the cloth-like tension in the house, the Winslow's annual end of summer camping trip was still on. Part of me was ecstatic, even though I had become skillful at acting like I hated living there. The thought of going camping for the first time filled me with genuine excitement, something I hadn't felt in a while. I clung to it like a lifeline, letting it distract me from the growing dread of starting over at yet another new school in just a few weeks. This time, I'd be entering sixth grade, a milestone year. But to me, it just meant more unfamiliar hallways, new faces and the same old fear of not belonging. My attempt to conceal my childlike innocence failed spectacularly during that trip, resulting in my becoming the butt of jokes for the teenagers and my foster parents.

Around the campfire that evening, the oldest foster girl, Janelle, told me an almost magical tale about a soft, furry creature that lived amongst the redwoods. She continued by explaining that if someone were to catch one of these rare creatures, they would bond with them and the tiny animal would be a lifelong pet. As I looked around in disbelief, the other girls agreed and nodded. Still a bit confused, I looked at Josephine and Elliot for confirmation. Josephine smiled and continued to puff on her cigarette, and Elliot cosigned Janelle's almost unbelievable story.

He began with, "They're called Worby's, and you can only catch them at night using a flashlight and calling out, "Here Worby, here Worby!"

"What's the flashlight for?" I inquired.

"When you hear them scurry around, shine the light at it and when you see its eyes, they will connect with you and come up to you to pick them up."

The truly naive, fairy tale believing little girl in me longed for the dependable connection only a Worby could offer. I set off into the woods, high hopes and flashlight in hand. I searched and searched until my fingers and toes felt like popsicles in the chilly night air. Making my way back to the distant campfire, I couldn't help but feel like this was just one more thing to add to the list of failures I had racked up as the disappointing eleven-year-old I was.

I choked back the tears, as I stepped into the campfire's light and mumble, "I couldn't find one."

A single tear had escaped and in my attempt to wipe it before anyone noticed, I flung my hand up to my face, immediately being reminded of the flashlight within my frozen grasp. The pain from the hit buried my tears and sent the familiar wave of embarrassment to warm my cheeks, confirming that I can't do anything right.

"Worby's are not real, idiot," one of them snarled.

In unison, the girls, along with my foster parents, exploded in laughter. Janelle, the oldest teen who was the ringleader of this terrible prank, laughed so hard she bent over and could barely continue to make coherent jokes about my level of stupidity. Josephine tossed her cigarette into the fire as she forcefully coughed in between, laughing. The humiliation cut deep, and my trust shattered even further. It was a final blow to my dwindling innocence, a bitter lesson that trust was a fool's game.

I adapted quickly. From then on, I only trusted myself and embraced being a loner, no matter how much I wanted to fit in somewhere, anywhere. The worthlessness settled into my bones, a familiar ache that whispered I wasn't deserving of love or stability. Looking back, I realized that leaving Grandma Dee's home had set off a chain reaction, a domino effect that would shape my sense of self-worth for years to come. Losing innocence, trust, and stability created scars that would take a lifetime to heal.

By the time I started my fourth elementary school in just two years, the weight of constant uprooting had taken a toll on me in ways I couldn't yet articulate. Each move felt like a silent erasure, of friendships, of routines, of any fragile sense of belonging I had pieced together in the short time before it was all packed up and left behind. I'd barely learn the teacher's name or find the courage to raise my hand in class before I was whisked away to another unfamiliar building filled with unfamiliar faces.

With every new school came a fresh wave of anxiety. I had to figure out the unspoken social rules all over again, who to sit next to, who not to look at, how to fade in just enough to avoid ridicule but not disappear completely. Survival, I learned rapidly, depended on conformity, not self-expression. I became a master at reading the room, adjusting myself like a chameleon, shrinking or stretching to match whatever version of me seemed safest.

Emotionally, I felt lost and disconnected. Like a boat constantly set adrift, never given time to anchor anywhere. I missed out on the consistency that gives kids a sense of identity, familiar hallways, the comfort of routine, the security of being known. I carried this invisible exhaustion with me every day, a low hum of grief for the stability I never had and the friendships I couldn't keep.

Each new classroom was another reminder that I was the outsider. That everyone already had their friends, their rhythm, and their inside jokes, and I was always starting from scratch. It was lonely, disorienting, and quietly devastating.

But in that quiet devastation, something else grew: resilience. A grit that came from learning to navigate change, to survive instability, and eventually, to adapt. I didn't know it then, but every move, every awkward introduction and lunch eaten alone, was slowly building the strength I would one day rely on to face far greater storms.

CHAPTER 15

BEYOND PARENTAL CONTROL

EVERY OTHER WEEKEND HAD become a precious routine, a fleeting glimpse of normalcy in a life otherwise defined by havoc and uncertainty. CPS was working to reunite me with Mama, and the weekend visits loosely knitted our fractured family back together. The anticipation started early each Friday, my heart pounding as I waited for Mama's sunflower-yellow station wagon to turn the corner onto my temporary street. When she arrived, her smile was bright but tinged with exhaustion, the weight of her world barely masked beneath her wide grin. This weekend felt different. Instead of heading straight to Mama's cramped Orangevale apartment, she surprised me with a detour.

"We're going to Grandma and Grandpa Brooks' house," she announced, her voice carrying a rare note of excitement.

I glanced at her curiously but didn't ask questions. Any change in scenery was a welcome break from the uninviting routine of the foster home. As we pulled into the driveway, nothing seemed out of the ordinary. The front yard looked as unassuming as ever, but then I heard it: laughter, cheers, and the unmistakable sound of splashing water coming from the backyard. Mama took my hand and led me through the side gate. What greeted me on the other side was nothing short of magical. Mama had arranged a surprise pool party for me. Brightly colored streamers and balloons swayed in the warm breeze, and the backyard was alive with family, friends, and the joy I hadn't felt in a long time.

"Surprise!" they shouted in unison, their voices echoing above the playful squeals of children already diving into the pool.

My jaw dropped, and for a moment, the daily heaviness I carried disappeared. In its place was pure, unfiltered happiness. I didn't know what to do first. There were water balloon relays, towering plates of food, and a massive cake decorated with my favorite cartoon characters. For the first time in what felt like forever, I felt seen, celebrated, and, most importantly, like a normal kid.

I dove into the festivities with everything I had, laughing until my side hurt as we tossed water balloons back and forth in a chaotic relay race. I savored the taste of grilled hot dogs and sweet lemonade, feeling a rare sense of belonging with each bite. When the heat became too much, I cannon-balled into the pool, the cool water washing away more than just the summer sweat. It cleansed parts of my soul. For a few blissful hours, I forgot I was a foster child waiting for social workers to decide her fate or the kid trying to piece together a broken identity. I was just me.

One of the most unexpected highlights of the party was Mama's friend Thomas. I met him a few times during weekend visits to her apartment. He was a lanky man with kind eyes and a youthful energy that set him apart from Curtis or my Dad. Thomas was an artist, and I'd spent hours during weekend visits watching him bring characters to life on paper. He'd patiently teach me to draw, showing me how to hold the pencil just right to create shadow and depth. I still cherish the drawings he'd given me, carefully folded and tucked away like treasures.

Yet, more than his talent, I loved the way Thomas made Mama laugh. Her laughter was a rare sound, like the fleeting trill of a bird you never expect to hear. It was light, genuine, and for a moment, it felt like the cracks in our lives had been sealed. I watched them from a distance. Thomas gestured animatedly near the grill while Mama covered her mouth, trying to stifle a laugh. Watching her face light up in that moment made me happy, and it gave me a strange sense of hope.

As the sun dipped lower, painting the sky in hues of gold and pink, I sat wrapped in a towel, watching the shadows stretch across the yard. The party was winding down, but I wanted to bottle up the laughter and warmth, to cling to this fleeting happiness for as long as I could. I didn't know what the future held. For now, however, this moment was mine.

When the party ended, we climbed into Mama's old station wagon and drove back to the tiny two-bedroom apartment she called home. It was a stark contrast to the sprawling estate where we lived together last, a house with a pool and eight acres to roam. That also came with abuse and betrayal. Still, the transition to this pint-sized apartment was jarring. The tight quarters, shared rooms, and constant noise from neighbors were an adjustment, to say the least. My brother and sister shared one bedroom while Mama and I squeezed into the other. The walls seemed to close in on us, and the place felt perpetually crowded, but it was ours.

Reflecting on those moments, I grasp what it must have been like for Mama. She had gone from running a family business to barely getting by on welfare, food stamps, and help from local food banks. It wasn't until I faced my own struggles decades later that I understood. Rebuilding my life after a divorce, surprisingly, helped me appreciate even a fraction of her struggle.

CPS monitored our family's progress through consistent weekend visits, starting bi-weekly and escalating to weekly. Mama worked tirelessly to finalize her divorce from Curtis and meet all the requirements to bring me home permanently. After two years in foster care, my mother regained custody of me in January 1993, when I was eleven. The transition was anything but smooth.

Starting at Ottoman Elementary mid-year was like being dropped into a foreign country. I struggled to fit in as much, if not more, than I had at my previous schools. I was desperate to have just one friend, someone who stuck around. The new neighborhood was unfamiliar, and I felt like an outsider wherever I went. I wasn't just trying to fit into a school; I was trying to piece together a life that felt whole, a daunting task for a child already carrying the weight of the world.

When I left Mama to enter foster care, I was a timid, scared little girl. By the time I returned, that girl was long gone. In her place stood a rebellious, angry preteen shaped by the pandemonium of bouncing between foster homes. I learned from the teens in my last foster home how to get loud and turn belligerence into an art form. Bitterness and rebellion had taken root deep within me, and I had no problem mouthing off to anyone: adults, neighbors, even family, if they so much as crossed me. I had grown wild, defiant, and completely unafraid to pick fights, even with grown women.

In our apartment complex, there were two grown sisters, Laura and Valerie, who were impossible to ignore. Laura was kind-hearted, with a vibrant smile despite the rotting teeth in her mouth. She introduced me to classic rock, and thanks to her, Aerosmith's "Crazy" and "Janie's Got a Gun" became staples of my makeshift soundtrack along with other great hits. Laura radiated a gentleness I admired.

Her sister Valerie, however, was another story. Valerie was blunt, cruel, and always had a snide remark for me. She outweighed me by at least four times and carried her weight with intimidating confidence. The tension between us was immediate and mutual. She talked trash every time she saw me outside, and I made it a point to fire back, aiming directly at her insecurities. It became our routine, a toxic back-and-forth that simmered until the day it boiled over.

There came a day when Valerie's merciless stream of insults pushed me past my breaking point. Her words, sharp and cruel, pierced through the fragile patience I had left. My fists clenched tightly as the heat rose to my face, a fiery mix of anger and defiance surging through me. Before I knew it, I was standing in the parking lot next to Mama's station wagon, my voice rising to meet hers. Valerie was three spaces down, unloading groceries from her car. I didn't hold back.

"You're just a fat jerk!" I shouted, the words spilling out before I could think twice. My voice wavered slightly, but I tried to inject as much confidence as I could muster.

The insult hit its mark. Valerie froze, her hand gripping a bag of groceries midair. Her face contorted with anger as she slowly placed the bag back in the car. Without a word, she marched toward me, her massive frame casting an imposing shadow. I stood my ground, but my heart pounded like a drum in my chest.

"Say it again," she spat, her voice trembling, not with fear, but with anger.

I swallowed hard, my mouth suddenly dry, but I refused to back down. "You're a fat jerk," I quivered, my voice barely above a whisper this time.

The words escaped with a flicker of defiance, even as I felt my knees weaken.

Valerie's expression darkened instantly; her smirk replaced with a glare that sent a chill down my spine. The air between us was electric, charged with tension and the undeniable certainty that this confrontation was about to escalate. Without hesitation, her massive hands shot out and shoved me hard against the car. The metal groaned under the impact, and the force rattled through my ribs. My breath caught, but the fire in me burned hotter. Fueled by pure adrenaline and fury, I launched myself back at her, swinging wildly. My fists connected, but it was like punching a mattress: my blows barely made a dent against her massive frame.

Valerie stood her ground, absorbing every hit with an almost amused defiance. Her size and strength dwarfed mine, but my rage wouldn't let me back down. I kept swinging, each punch less effective than the last until my arms felt like dead weights. Exhaustion overtook me, and I stumbled back, panting and defeated. Valerie stared at me, her expression a mix of annoyance and pity.

"You done?" she sneered, brushing off her shirt as if I'd only flicked lint from her shoulder.

Humiliated and fuming, I stormed off to our apartment, nursing my bruised pride. My emotions boiled over as I recounted the incident to Mama, choking on tears of frustration.

"She shoved me against the car, Mama! She thinks she can do whatever she wants because she's older!" My words tumbled out in a mix of anger and desperation.

Mama's face shifted, her expression hardening in a way that sent a shiver down my spine. She said little, but the way she bolted out the door spoke louder than words ever could. I trailed behind her, my heart pounding, unsure of what was about to happen but knowing it would be explosive. We found Valerie standing outside her apartment, still smug from our earlier altercation. Mama wasted no time. She stepped right up to her, her voice sharp and unwavering.

"You put your hands on my daughter?" she demanded, her tone laced with irritation.

Valerie stammered, clearly surprised by Mama's intensity. "She started it," Valerie stated, trying to shift the blame.

"She's eleven years old and I don't care who started it," Mama snapped. "You ever lay a finger on my daughter again, and I'll make sure you see the inside of a jail cell for a long time. Do you hear me?"

Her words were like steel, cutting through any defense Valerie might have mustered.

The entire apartment complex seemed to hold its breath. Neighbors peeked through curtains and cracked open their doors, captivated by the showdown. Mama stood her ground, her presence radiating a protective ferocity I hadn't seen in a long time. She wasn't just defending me; she was reclaiming her role as my protector in a world that often felt like it was against us.

Valerie mumbled an apology, her bravado shrinking under Mama's unyielding glare. Satisfied but still seething, Mama turned on her heel, grabbing my arm firmly as we walked back to our apartment. Inside, Mama sat me down and looked me straight in the eye.

"Tina, stop mouthing off to adults and trying to fight people! You understand me? If someone messes with you, you come to me. I'll handle it. You just need to stay out of trouble."

Watching Mama go into full "Mama Bear" mode was a moment I clung to, a rare flash of safety and validation in a world that often felt unsafe and unforgiving. I felt seen, protected, and loved, even if the feeling didn't last as long as I wished it would.

As proud as I was of Mama in that moment, standing up for me against Valerie, it also stirred a painful question: why hadn't she reacted that way when Curtis hurt me? The resentment was twisted and deep, born from the countless times I needed her protection, but didn't get it in the way I had hoped. I knew she tried. She'd stepped in, yelled at him, even physically intervened, but Curtis would retaliate, hitting her or screaming in her face until her strength crumbled under his rage.

I finally understood when I found myself in a similar situation as an adult. I struggled to stand up for myself, tangled in fear and self-doubt, even though I knew I desperately needed to leave a violent relationship. It was during one of those moments of helplessness that an insight hit me: was this what Mama felt? Had she fought the same internal battles, knowing she needed to escape but feeling trapped and powerless? I imagine she did. That realization softened some of my resentment, replacing it with bittersweet empathy. Mama wasn't weak; she was human, and like me, she had her own struggles, ones that I was only beginning to comprehend. It wasn't until I became a mother myself that I began to understand and forgive the distance that once existed between Mama and me. With each passing year and every challenge of raising my own children, my respect, love and empathy for her deepened. In time, that understanding bridged the gap between us, and thankfully, we found our way back to each other. Still, as a preteen, I kept Mama on her toes, my constant antics giving her more than enough to handle.

Despite her efforts to guide and discipline me, I was slipping further beyond her control. CPS limited her ability to discipline me by monitoring her every move. Spankings, which might have been effective at this stage, were entirely off the table. The result was a volatile household where my anger festered unchecked.

My Aunt Miranda came over to visit a few weekends later. Miranda was closer to my age than most aunts, only four years older than me, and we had a bond more like sisters. We loved confusing people when we introduced ourselves.

"No, she's not my cousin, this is my Aunt Miranda," I'd say proudly.

Her presence usually brought laughter, but that day, it brought anarchy. Mama had run to the corner store, leaving Miranda and me at the apartment. We'd been running around the complex, burning off energy, when we headed back inside for a glass of Tang. Miranda got to the door first and, with a mischievous grin, locked me out.

At first, I laughed it off, pounding on the door playfully. "Come on, Miranda, let me in!"

When she smirked through the kitchen window, shaking her head no, my irritation bubbled. "I'm serious. Open the door," I said, my voice rising.

Her laughter only grew louder. "What are you going to do, Tina?" she teased.

"I'm going to break the window if you don't let me in." My face grew hot, and my fists clenched as anger surged through me like a storm. "Open the stupid door!" I shouted through gritted teeth.

Miranda leaned closer to the window, her expression daring me. "I bet you won't," she said with a raised brow.

Her words struck a nerve, and that was it. The rage I'd been bottling up erupted. I drew back my fist and slammed it into the glass. The kitchen window shattered into a spray of jagged shards, raining down onto the counter and the kitchen table where Mama had prepped dinner. Miranda jumped back in shock; her laughter replaced by wide-eyed terror.

Blood trickled down my hand, the sting registering a second too late. The sound of Mama's station wagon pulling into the lot brought me back to reality. My hand hung limp at my side, droplets of blood pooling on the ground. Panic set in as I realized what I'd done. A neighbor told Mama in the parking lot that I had broken a window.

Mama's footsteps pounded up the stairs. "What the hell happened?" she asked, her voice sharp with concern as her eyes darted between my bloody hand and the shattered window.

"Miranda locked me out," I muttered, still trembling with adrenaline and regret.

Mama grabbed the nearest dish towel and wrapped it tightly around my hand. "Why on earth would you punch a window, Tina?" she demanded, her frustration mingling with worry as she inspected my injuries.

Thankfully, my cuts were superficial, but her disappointment stung more than the glass.

As Mama rinsed my hand under the faucet, her voice softened. "You've got to get control of this anger, Tina. You can't keep letting it rule you."

Miranda stood in the corner, unusually quiet, as Mama turned her attention to her. "And you locking her out? What were you thinking?"

Dinner that night was a far cry from the homemade meal Mama had planned. The shards of glass ruined the prepped food, so we settled for bologna sandwiches with government cheese, apple slices, and milk. As we sat at the table, the air was heavy with unspoken tension. My hand throbbed, a painful reminder of how far I'd let my anger take me.

Miranda came around less and less after my outburst, leaving a noticeable gap in my small world of companionship. Her absence created an aching void and set me on a mission to find new friendships amongst the other children in our apartment complex. That's when I first noticed the girl I'd later come to know as Gabriella or Ella, as she preferred. Ella intrigued me in ways I couldn't quite explain at the time. She was a quiet presence, always composed, a stark contrast to her hectic surroundings. Her family was comprised of four younger brothers, who were an endless source of noise and energy. Despite the pandemonium they created, Ella never seemed to lose her cool. She was a lighthouse in the middle of a raging sea, skillfully guiding her brothers through the courtyard and into their apartment with a serene authority that fascinated me.

I'd see her occasionally, but never enough to satisfy my curiosity. Why didn't she play outside like the rest of the kids? Why wasn't she ever at the bus stop in the mornings? Most importantly, how had she managed to avoid school altogether? The mystery surrounding her was palpable, and I was determined to uncover her secrets.

The laundry room became my makeshift mission control. Mama must have been baffled by my sudden eagerness to help with the laundry. However, I had a strategy: I'd wait for Ella to appear, basket in hand, and create an opportunity to talk to her. One afternoon, my patience paid off. I saw her heading to the laundry room as I returned from school. Without a second thought, I darted upstairs, swapped my backpack for a half-filled basket of laundry, grabbed a handful of quarters from Mama's laundry jar, and hurried back down.

Barely paying attention, I loaded the washer with clothes, dropped in the quarters, and slammed the lid shut, trying to look as nonchalant as possible. Ella, perched casually on one of the dryers with a book in hand, didn't even glance up. Then, without missing a beat, she said,

"Aren't you going to add washing powder?"

"Oh, shoot!" I blurted, feeling embarrassed.

Looking up from her book, with a small smile, she gestured toward the box of detergent in her basket. "Here, you can use some of mine."

It was the perfect icebreaker, and that small moment of generosity was the beginning of a friendship that would shape my childhood in ways I hadn't expected. A friendship that would last for years to come. Ella formally introduced herself, and I learned that she and her family lived in one of the three-bedroom apartments downstairs. Something Mama explained had been unavailable when she desperately needed an apartment to get me back from foster care.

Ella was strikingly beautiful. Her long, curly dark brown hair was unlike anything I'd seen, and she explained that in her family, women didn't cut their hair. Her mother, Patricia, also had long, flowing hair, although hers was a fiery red that complimented her piercing blue eyes. Ella had a unique Brazilian tan, warm brown eyes, and a mole perfectly placed between her nose and upper lip that added to her charm.

As naturally nosy as I was, I asked about her father. "He's Mexican," she said matter-of-factly.

"Oh, so that's why your skin is darker," I responded, completely unaware of how ignorant I sounded. Then I added, "My dad's Black, but he's light Black, so I didn't get any color from him."

Ella looked puzzled for a moment before I barreled on with another question.

"Why haven't I ever seen your dad?"

"He's in prison," she said, her tone flat but not ashamed.

"Why is he in jail?" I asked, wide-eyed.

She patiently clarified, "He's not in jail. He's in prison. Jail is for a short time, and prison is when you have to stay for years and years."

"Why is he in prison?" I pressed; my curiosity was unrelenting.

Ella hesitated before leaning in slightly and whispering, "My mom says when people ask that, I should tell them it's none of their business. Just between you and me, he got caught stealing."

From that moment, Ella and I were inseparable. She quickly became my most cherished friend. We spent every free moment together, but there were limits to where we could hang out. I was too embarrassed to invite her over to our apartment. Sharing a room with Mama and a living room often occupied by my younger siblings left little space for company. Her home had similar constraints, so our playground became the outdoors or, on rainy days, the laundry room.

The rebellious "Bad Girl" persona I had adopted during my time in foster care didn't sit well with Ella's mother. She often seemed uneasy about Ella spending too much time with me, her protective instincts kicking in. Despite her reservations, Ella and I still carved out moments to be together. Ella's family volunteered with an organization that raised funds for families of inmates, a cause close to their hearts. One way they raised money was by creating and selling handmade beaded necklaces, beautiful, intricate pieces of jewelry that were more than simple beads strung on a cord. These weren't store-bought beads; they were works of art. Each bead was handcrafted with care, shaped, designed, and painted by hand, transforming raw materials into unique and vibrant jewelry. Ella, always resourceful and eager to find ways for us to hang out, convinced her mom to let me join by teaching me the art of bead-making. It was her way of bridging the gap between my wild energy and her mother's need for reassurance.

As someone who naturally loved crafting, I embraced the opportunity wholeheartedly. We would sit for hours at the small kitchen table in her family's apartment, cutting, rolling, and shaping soft clay into perfectly uniform beads. It required focus and patience, which at first felt foreign to me, but Ella's calm demeanor had a way of grounding me. She'd show me how to use simple tools to create delicate patterns or grooves, and I quickly learned to mimic her steady hands.

Once the beads were baked and hardened, the real fun began with painting them. We mixed colors, experimenting with bold, vibrant hues and intricate designs. The table would be covered in tiny pots of paint, brushes of all sizes, and beads drying in neat rows. Each one was a tiny masterpiece, and seeing the transformation from raw clay to finished product was deeply satisfying. For me, it wasn't just about making jewelry; it was a rare opportunity to channel my restless energy into something productive and beautiful.

I felt a sense of peace I rarely experienced, surrounded by the hum of her family and the quiet rhythm of our craft. It was more than just bead-making; it was a connection between Ella and me, between creativity and purpose, and between the disorderly parts of myself and the calm I so desperately craved. Mrs. Patricia, though still weary of my rebellious streak, softened as she saw my dedication to the craft. For a few hours at a time, I wasn't the troubled kid from upstairs. I was just a girl, learning to create something beautiful with my hands and sharing in Ella's world.

Staying true to my nature, I convinced Ella to go to the corner store with me to buy beer and drink it at the local park. Ella gave me the look you give someone who's completely lost their mind.

"It's called O'Doul's. It's beer, but not beer," I explained enthusiastically, "and anyone can buy it," only confusing her more.

"How is it beer if it's not beer?" Ella stated matter-of-factly.

"I don't know, I just heard anyone can buy it and it tastes like beer. Let's try it."

Ella sighed, shook her head, and gave me a resigned shrug. "Do you even have money for this?"

"Yep!" I replied confidently, conveniently leaving out the part where I'd swiped five dollars from Mama's purse while she was in the shower. She didn't ask, and I wasn't about to offer that little detail.

We strutted into the corner store, trying to look as casual as two middle-schoolers trying to buy beer could manage. The cashier's eyes locked on us the moment we walked in, his suspicion practically radiating across the store. I was used to it by now. Most of the time, I came in to grab a candy bar (or three) that accidentally found their way into my pockets. This was different, though. This time, I wasn't here for candy; I was here for beer. Well, sort of.

We made our way to the beer coolers, scanning the shelves like two detectives on a high-stakes mission. There it was: a green cardboard carrier with six glass bottles of O'Doul's, practically glowing like a prize in a claw machine. Ella and I exchanged a glance, a mix of nerves and thrill, before I reached out and grabbed two bottles, feeling the chill of the glass against my fingers.

At the register, we placed the bottles on the counter and looked up at the cashier, who met us with a withering stare. His eyebrows were furrowed, his lips pressed tight, and his entire demeanor screamed disapproval. My heart started pounding. What was he going to do? Ban us from the store? Call Mama? Or worse, the cops?

"You can't take out two," he said flatly, shattering my panic spiral with his deadpan tone. "You have to buy the entire pack."

Relieved but still jittery, I darted back to the cooler to grab the half-empty carrier. Ella carefully returned the stray bottles to their spots while I placed the full six-pack on the counter. The cashier's unimpressed gaze didn't waver.

"Five twenty-seven," he said in a tone that suggested he couldn't believe he was wasting his time on this transaction.

Panic set in again. "I only have five dollars," I whispered, turning to Ella with wide eyes. "Do you have any change?"

She fished through her pockets and came up with a single, solitary quarter. "That's all I've got," she said apologetically.

With a line now forming behind us, I could feel the judgmental eyes of the customers boring into the back of my neck. I scanned the floor, hoping for a miracle in the form of two pennies, when I spotted the "Leave a Penny, Take a Penny" tray on the counter. Jackpot! Exactly two pennies sat there, as if the universe had aligned just for this moment. I proudly handed over the five dollars, quarter, and two pennies, grinning like I'd just won the lottery. The cashier sighed heavily, rang us up, and shoved the six-pack across the counter.

We grabbed the beer and bolted for the door, giggling like we'd just pulled off the heist of the century.

"I can't believe we just bought beer!" I exclaimed, barely able to contain my excitement.

Before the door could even close behind us, the cashier's familiar, irritated voice called after us. "It's not real beer! It's fake beer!" His words barely registered. We were too busy basking in our triumphant moment.

We made our way to the park, each clutching a bottle like a trophy. With a dramatic flourish, we twisted off the caps. Then we took a big swig. Instant regret. The taste hit us like a slap: cold, metallic, tangy, and just...wrong. My face scrunched up in disgust, while Ella stuck her tongue out repeatedly, as if she could scrub the flavor off her taste buds.

"This is disgusting," I said, my voice muffled by my attempt not to gag.

Ella nodded. Her expression was a mix of horror and betrayal. "Who drinks this on purpose?" she asked, shaking her head.

We burst into laughter, doubled over on the park bench, as we set the bottles down with finality. Our grand beer adventure had turned into a comedic disaster, but it was a memory we'd laugh about for years. We dumped the rest of the beer into the park trash can and headed back to our apartment complex, laughing the entire way home. Turns out, we didn't need fake beer to act like rebels. The adventures and the bond we shared were enough.

In Ella, I found more than just a friend; I found an anchor in a stormy sea. She brought a sense of stability to my otherwise out-of-control life, a steady presence that felt like a warm hug on the coldest days. She became my confidante, someone I could trust with the messy, jagged edges of my story without fear of judgment. Her kindness was a salve to my wounds, her calm demeanor a reminder that not everything in life had to be frantic or overwhelming. Ella embodied everything I admired but often felt I lacked: calm, patience, and a quiet strength that seemed unshakable. She carried herself with a grace that masked her young age, managing the frenzy of her younger brothers with an ease I envied. While I lashed out at the world, she approached life with a kind of grounded resilience, showing me that strength didn't always have to be loud or defiant.

Though our circumstances were far from perfect, our friendship became a beacon in the darkness. Her laughter had a way of cutting through my anger, and her steadiness often made me feel braver than I thought I could be. She reminded me, in her quiet way, that I wasn't as alone as I felt, that even in the midst of pain and uncertainty, connection was possible. Her friendship didn't just make the instability of my life more bearable; it gave me hope. She was a bright spot in a world that often felt bleak, a source of light that reminded me there was still good to be found, even in the most unexpected places. Through her, I saw that while life might never be easy; it didn't have to be faced entirely alone.

"I survived because the fire inside me burned brighter than the fire around me."
— Joshua Graham

PART 4

MILESTONES

CHAPTER 16

REJECTED AND RESILIENT

THE STREETLIGHTS COMING ON determined Ella's curfew, and she usually spent her weekends visiting her dad in prison and attending church, which left me with plenty of time by myself. So, I did what I knew to do best, which was integrate myself into someone's family and I had the perfect family in mind. The Zamora family lived in the apartment next to the laundry room. Ella and I called the Zamora family, "The Spanish Family." Even though Ella was Mexican, she did not speak Spanish. The Zamora family only spoke Spanish and only listened to Spanish music. Ella and I would hang out in the laundry room and listen to the mariachi music through the walls and make up words to go with the beat, since we did not know what they were singing. The Zamora's were a family of six, two daughters and two sons, accompanied by their parents. My limited knowledge of any culture, let alone Hispanic culture, convinced me that Mexican women may not cut their hair, since the Zamora mother and daughters also had very long hair.

The Zamora's and many of their friends and family would hang out in the grass area next to their apartment beside the laundry room, listening to music, dancing, and best of all, barbecuing. However, the stuff they grilled differed from what my grandpa grilled. There were no hamburgers or hotdogs on their grills. They had this weird thin flat-looking meat, jalapenos, corn on the cob and tortillas. My favorite part of their regular parties was when one man would shout in a high pitched, rhythmic noise that I later learned was a "Grito," a vocal expression often used to convey joy and excitement, and the other men would follow almost challenging each other to see who can yell the loudest and longest. The neighbors hated it and complained, but my intrigue compelled me to seek an invitation to their amazing festivals.

There was nothing subtle about my ways. I would literally stand by the corner of the apartment and stare, taking in all the excitement, fun, and delicious smells. Finally, the daughters took pity on me and motioned for me to come over, during which time I became shy and hesitated until their motions became more aggressive and purposeful. Making my way over to the daughters, Veronica and Rosa would start a rather interesting game of charades as I attempted to learn Spanish words, and they attempted to understand what I was saying. My saving grace was Rosa, the youngest daughter. She was the family's English spokesperson. She spoke very limited English and would attempt to translate for anyone trying to communicate to the Gringos, as they would call us. At first there was a bit of a learning curve, but my determination would outlast a language barrier. Now I want to say I learned fluent Spanish and communicated effectively, but truthfully, my Spanish was limited, so Rosa became my translator.

The Zamora family welcomed me with open arms, even giving me a nickname "Narizona." I felt special and accepted, even though my Spanish was weak and their English was just as bad. The universal language of hugs and smiles filled my soul with an acceptance I had only ever felt with my Grandmother Marilyn and Grandpa Gio. It didn't take long for me to learn that "Narizona" meant "enormous nose", but by that point I didn't care. The Zamora family won my heart and set in motion a healing that I didn't recognize. I fell in love with their culture, their delicious food, and the thin meat that I learned was Carne Asada is now my favorite thing to eat. The Zamora family embraced me and tried to teach me how to dance and "Grito." I was never too good at it, but had fun trying.

Although the first part of the year started out roughly, I was glad to be home with my family. I made a new friend, Ella, found an honorary spot in the Zamora family, and was now about to start middle school. Things were looking up, and I had a sense of optimism. Life had finally slowed down enough for me to imagine something better.

Discovering that my new school divided students into teams named after animals, I felt thrilled to join the Peacocks team. Peacocks reminded me of our old family home, the land where they wandered freely, their vivid feathers fanned out like nature's fireworks. It was one of my oldest and happiest childhood memories. Somehow, being a peacock felt like a sign that middle school would be a fresh start, one that I desperately needed.

The first week of school was a whirlwind of faces and names, but one stood out immediately. Seth. He had a confident swagger that was hard to ignore. His long black hair brushed his shoulders, and he wore oversized pants paired with chunky skater shoes. His skateboard was practically an extension of his body, always with him as he zipped to and from school. What caught my attention most, though, were his nails, painted black. I'd never seen a boy do that before.

We clicked right away. Seth and I became tetherball partners during recess, our competitive spirits aligning perfectly as we took turns smashing the yellow ball with such force; our wrists bearing the marks of our victories. He was my in-school bestie, the type of friend who made the days feel shorter and the laughter endless. Life felt almost perfect. I had Mama, stability, friends outside of school, and now a school friend who made each day brighter. The illusion of perfection soon crumbled.

On a warm afternoon during recess, Seth and I sat on the curb near the tetherball courts, our conversation veering toward family. It was casual until I mentioned, "My dad's Black." The words felt natural to me, just a fact about my life. Seth froze. His relaxed demeanor vanished, replaced by something unrecognizable.

"What do you mean your dad's Black?" he asked, his voice tinged with disbelief. I stared at him, confused by his reaction.

"He's Black," I repeated, unsure of why it mattered.

Seth's face twisted in anger, his tone sharp as he spat out, "You're a nigger?"

The word hit me like a slap, the venom behind it making my chest tighten. My mind raced. How could he say something like that? He stood abruptly and walked away, leaving me sitting there, stunned and reeling.

The days that followed were a blur of humiliation and confusion. Cold indifference or outright hostility greeted me with every attempt to talk to Seth. He and his new group of friends took joy in tormenting me. "Wigger," "Nigger Lover," "Big Bird," "Nigger Lips," and "Magilla

Gorilla" became their go-to insults. Each name they hurled stung like a bee sting, the pain lingering long after the words faded.

School, which had once felt like a haven, became unbearable. I stopped going outside for recess, choosing instead to volunteer in classrooms, cutting construction paper or prepping projects for teachers. At lunch, I sat alone, shoveling food into my mouth as quickly as possible so I could escape the cafeteria. The laughter and chatter that once surrounded me now felt like a cruel reminder of my isolation.

I didn't understand. How could someone hate me for who I was? Before that moment, racism had been something abstract, a concept I'd heard very little about. Now, its truth was undeniable and stared me in the face, raw and unrelenting, the weight pressing down on me in a way I couldn't escape. Seth's words still rang in my ears, a cruel echo that refused to fade. I wasn't just Christina anymore; I was a label, a slur, something to be cast aside and ridiculed. Was this why Curtis hated me? The question gnawed at me. Was it my heritage, my father, my existence, something deeper I couldn't grasp? I felt as though my whole life's rejection had condensed into a single moment of clarity. For the first time, I saw the lines society drew around people, the walls that kept them divided, and the barriers that I, somewhere in between, would never fully fit into.

As a child, I always felt out of place, like a puzzle piece in the wrong box, forced into shapes that didn't quite fit. My white side treated me like I was the black sheep, too different to fully embrace. Family gatherings on that side were a constant reminder of my otherness, their stares lingering for a moment too long, their questions thinly veiled judgments. On the other hand, my Black relatives saw me as something else entirely. "You're so bougie," they'd say, their laughter tinged with teasing, but their words carrying an edge. "Stuck up," they'd call me, pointing out the way I spoke or the things I liked, as though my preferences disqualified me from belonging. They made it clear I wasn't one of them either, and the wounds from their words lingered long after the laughter faded.

The rejection felt suffocating. It was as if I were floating in limbo, trapped between two worlds that refused to claim me. I was too Black for the white kids, too white for the Black kids. It became the refrain of my life, a melody I couldn't escape. I spent so much time just trying to find my place, my people, the ones who would embrace me for who I was, not what I was.

The rejection left scars, ones I would carry with me long into adulthood. Even as I grew older and understood the complexities of race and identity, the wounds remained tender. Every sideways glance, every offhand comment, every moment of being overlooked or singled out brought those feelings rushing back, a tidal wave of unworthiness threatening to drown me.

Amid the pain and confusion of not fitting in anywhere, I found resilience. It wasn't an easy resilience, the kind that comes naturally or without effort. Rejection, loneliness, and a stubborn refusal to give up on finding my people forged that resilience. That determination led me to Ella, and through her, to the Zamora family. Ella was my first genuine connection to the Hispanic community. Quiet and kind, she didn't see me as "too Black" or "too white." To her, I was simply her friend. Her best friend! The Zamora family extended that same sense of acceptance. They treated me like one of their own, inviting me into their home and lives with open arms. It didn't matter that I wasn't Mexican; it didn't matter that my skin didn't match theirs. What mattered was that I was there, and they welcomed me with warmth I hadn't known outside of Grandma Marilyn and Grandpa Gio's love.

In my most chaotic years, the Zamora family offered an escape. Their laughter, the smell of grilling Carne Asada, and the upbeat Spanish music created a comforting atmosphere. It was a world so different from the fractured spaces I'd known, and it felt like home. They had a way of pulling me in, making me part of their circle. For the first time in a long time, I felt seen, not for what I wasn't, but for who I was.

Middle school brought its own whirlwind of instability. I attended three middle schools in two years. I changed schools twice because of relocation; a third move was necessary after an incident with a male student following me into the bathroom, leaving me feeling unsafe and unsupported by the school's lack of disciplinary action. Each new start further uprooted me, making it harder to find solid footing. One thing remained constant, though: the sense of belonging I found within the Hispanic community. At each new school, I gravitated toward the Mexican children. Their way of folding me into their groups felt effortlessly natural. My presence went unquestioned, and they accepted me as though I was always meant to be there.

With my rebellious streak and desire to belong, it was only a matter of time before I found myself drawn to a local Mexican street gang. In actuality, they were a family, not just a group of bad boys. They looked out for one another, fiercely loyal and unapologetically bold. I respected their refusal to be pushed around. I even envied it. I wanted that kind of strength, that kind of protection. They didn't care that I wasn't Mexican. In fact, my heritage made me something of an anomaly, a unique addition to their circle. They joked I couldn't officially join because I wasn't Mexican, but that didn't stop them from treating me like I was. They gave me all the benefits of being part of their gang; protection, camaraderie, and a sense of belonging, with no strings attached.

At first, I thought it was just about the image. The bandanas, the swagger, the way they commanded respect wherever they went, it was intoxicating. As time went on, I realized it was something deeper. It was the way they showed up for each other, no questions asked. It was the way they embraced me, flaws and all, without making me feel like I had to prove anything. In a world where I was constantly trying to fit into spaces that didn't want me, they clarified I was enough, just as I was. I never feared gang life. Contrary to expectations, I remained unafraid even during dangerous situations, fights, or while being chased and shot at. I trusted them. They made me feel safe in a way I hadn't experienced before. More than a gang, they were my family, and for the first time in a long time, I didn't feel alone.

Upon reflection, I can see how these connections shaped me. The Zamora's, Ella, and the gang all taught me that belonging doesn't always look the way one expects to. It doesn't have to come from the people who share your blood or even your culture. Sometimes, it comes from the people who see you, who accept you, and who make room for you in their world. Those middle school years were far from perfect. They were unstable, messy, and filled with their own set of challenges. I also experienced joy, connection, and increasing resilience during that time of my life, which helped me persevere. The Hispanic community gave me a place to land when I felt like I was floating in limbo, and for that, I will always be grateful. They showed me that belonging isn't about fitting in; it's about finding the people who make you feel at home.

CHAPTER 17
INNOCENCE TAKEN

LEAVING ORANGEVALE TO MOVE closer to Mama's new job was bittersweet, a double-edged sword of relief and sorrow. Michael, Angela and I followed her to a small apartment near her work. As we packed up, I hoped for a fresh start, but deep down it felt like another chapter in our cycle of instability. On one hand I was glad to escape the constant bullying at school, but on the other hand, the thought of leaving Ella and the Zamora family left a hollow ache in my chest. Old Town Fair Oaks promised a fresh start, with its sprawling apartment complex, shimmering pool, and nearby shops. The pool became my new refuge, a place to retreat and disappear when life felt overwhelming. Between the local park, the pool, and the corner store, I didn't have to hide out in the laundry room anymore. Still, as much as I craved solitude, I wanted more. I wanted to fit in, to have friends, to feel like I belonged. Then came Derrick Stone.

He was a tall and slender white boy, with piercing blue eyes, a bit of scruffy facial hair, and a grin that oozed confidence. Derrick lived with his grandmother, who let him come and go as he pleased, making him the unofficial king of the courtyard. He and his friends, Jake and Eddie, were a whirlwind of energy, running through the complex, leaping over barriers, and doing back flips off benches. Derrick's presence was magnetic, and I found myself lingering on the balcony just to catch a glimpse of him.

Trying my hardest to think of something clever or witty to say when they ran by, I would end up calling out cheesy remarks like, "Don't hurt yourself!" or "Shouldn't you be in bed?" desperate for his attention. Each time, I'd cringe inwardly at how awkward I sounded, but eventually, I caught his eye.

"Hi," I said one evening, my voice overly enthusiastic.

"Hey," he replied smoothly, pausing to look up at me.

"What's your name?" I asked, masquerading ignorance even though I'd already learned it from Shannon Rae, the neighborhood gossip.

"Derrick," he answered, flashing that charming smile.

"Cool," I replied, trying to sound nonchalant, though my body tingled with excitement.

Derrick's rebellious confidence, with which he carried himself, had always attracted me. Moving through the world as if it belonged to him, he was a mix of charm and defiance. He and his friends tattooed each other in the laundry room, broke into cars, and vandalized the new homes behind our complex. His reckless behavior fascinated me, and I longed to be part of his circle. Not just a girl on the sidelines, but someone they saw and accepted.

I'll never forget the night Derrick finally invited me along. Jake, Eddie, two girls I didn't recognize, and I followed Derrick to the back of the complex. They had stacked paint buckets and wood scraps to scale the wall into the construction site. My heart raced with excitement as Derrick helped me climb over.

"We're going to get snacks," I heard Eddie call out as Derrick climbed over the wall.

I ignored the unease in my gut, desperate to prove I belonged, also a bit excited with the idea of possibly making out with Derrick. How romantic would it be for my first kiss to be under the majestic moonlight? My naive fairy tale would turn into a monstrous horror film, one you would have to be eighteen or older to rent.

The sharp scent of fresh paint hung in the air as we climbed through the window of a newly built home. Inside, Derrick gleefully pointed out the destruction he and his friends had caused: gaping holes punched into pristine walls, smears of paint defacing the carpet, and shards of drywall kicked in and scattered like confetti. He led me to the master bedroom, where a jagged, life-sized hole marred the wall, pink insulation spilling out in tufts like grotesque cotton candy.

"I did that myself," he announced with pride, his grin wide, as though he were presenting a masterpiece worthy of admiration.

I forced a weak smile, trying to match his enthusiasm, but my stomach tangled in knots. Guilt gnawed at me, sharp and ceaseless. *I don't belong here,* I thought, the words echoing in my mind. The destruction was overwhelming, too much to process. Even though I hadn't laid a hand on anything, simply standing there, surrounded by the destruction, made me feel complicit. The weight of responsibility settled heavily on my shoulders, as though by being present, I had become an accomplice to their senseless acts of vandalism.

Then, without warning, Derrick's lips crashed against mine. My stomach twisted. This wasn't what I wanted, this wasn't how it was supposed to feel. I had imagined something gentle, something safe. This felt like a robbery, not a kiss. His rough, chapped lips grated against mine, like gritty sandpaper, and his tongue forced its way into my mouth, intrusive and invasive, as if searching for something I didn't have to give. The stale taste of tobacco on his breath made me want to vomit. My heart pounded, not with excitement, but with a growing sense of dread. I froze, paralyzed by confusion and fear, unsure of how to react. His hands moved under my shirt, finding my training bra, and I flinched. His fingers were rough and cold against my skin, and shame surged through me like a fever. I wanted to disappear, to fold myself into nothing and vanish from beneath his hands.

"Stop," I said, my voice timid and unsure, a fragile plea that disappeared into the air between us. I wanted to scream it, to make it echo off the walls, but all that came out was a whisper. When he didn't stop, something inside me cracked. Wasn't "no" supposed to matter?

"Relax," he snapped, his tone cold, dismissive, and full of entitlement. "You know you want this."

Panic surged through me as his strength overpowered mine. He shoved me to the floor, pinning my wrists above my head with one hand while the other tugged at the waistband of my shorts. The air felt heavy, like it had been sucked out of the room, making it hard to breathe. My skin burned beneath his grip, but it was the sound of his breath in my ear, so calm, that terrified me. My pleas came flooding out.

"Stop! Please stop!" My words met with silence, as if they didn't exist.

My shorts slid down, leaving only my panties as a frail barrier, one I knew wouldn't protect me.

Anxious, I choked out, "I don't want to do this. I've never done this before," hoping my honesty might spark some shred of mercy in him. He didn't pause. "I want to go home!" I cried, tears streaming down my face as my voice broke under the weight of desperation.

His grip tightened, ignoring my sobs, my terror, my words, leaving me defenseless against the acts to come.

Pulling my panties to the side, he fumbled for a moment before an intense, searing pain erupted through me raw and mercilessly as a burning sensation radiated from my vagina into my belly, followed by sharp, lightning-like jolts. His body, heavy and unyielding like a pile of bricks, pressed down on me as he thrust harder and faster between my legs. The initial dry, tearing pain gave way to wet warmth, but the agony remained, consuming every part of me. I wanted to scream, to push him off, to fight back, but the memories of my powerless struggles against Curtis flooded my mind. His weight, his smothering presence, it always ended the same, with me unable to break free. My arms, once pushing against him with all the strength I had, grew weak, resistance fading into helpless surrender. My hands dropped in defeat, grasping at the carpet beneath me, clinging to its fibers with each agonizing thrust, as if holding on could somehow ground me in a moment that was spiraling out of control. Resistance felt useless. So, I did what I learned to do: I gave up. I retreated into the only refuge I had, my mind. Yet even in my mind, I couldn't escape. The bursts of pain yanked me back to reality, each one more excruciating than the last. I clenched my teeth to suppress the sobs threatening to escape and turned my head to the side, letting silent tears stream down my cheeks. The moonlight filtered through the window, illuminating my suffering, while offering no solace.

After what seemed like time had stopped, his grip on my wrist loosened, and he pushed himself off me. Derrick zipped up his pants without meeting my eyes, and then walked away in silence, leaving me shattered on the cold floor. He didn't even look at me. Like I wasn't a person. Just a thing he had used. That silence was louder than any insult. I lay there hollowed out, trying to convince myself I was still real.

My heart pounded and my mind went blank, unable to process what just happened. Eventually, I forced myself to sit up, my body trembling as I put my shorts back on. The shorts felt foreign against my skin, as if I were wearing someone else's clothes, someone who had just been broken. Stumbling through the darkened house, I followed the faint glow of moonlight, a light that should have cast a magical glow on a fairytale kiss. Instead, it poured through the window like a cruel witness to the horror I'd just suffered. When I reached the makeshift scaffolding, I hesitated, tears flowing like an unstoppable flood. I paused, gripping the structure, trying to steady myself. Years of practice had taught me well; I knew how to bury the pain, to force the tears back and trade them for the numbing emptiness that had become my armor. It was a skill I'd perfected, a survival tactic for when life's cruelties became too much to bear, and now it was the only way I could move forward.

Falling into the habit of zoning out and going through the motions became an almost invisible armor, shielding me from the overwhelming intensity of emotions I wasn't ready to face. It was a defense mechanism that, while helpful during challenging moments of my youth, clung to me like a shadow well into adulthood. Breaking free from that trance-like state, where the mind detaches while the body carries on, was one of the hardest internal battles I fought as an adult. It required a conscious effort to remain present, to engage fully with my surroundings, and to open myself up to feelings I had long avoided. The journey to unlearn this deeply ingrained habit was not just about staying present but about reclaiming parts of myself I had left behind in those moments of dissociation. It was a fight to be whole again, to live, rather than merely surviving.

A comforting silence greeted me as I zombie-like shuffled into our apartment. Mama and my siblings were asleep, oblivious to the storm raging inside me. Creeping through the dark, I made my way down the hall. The bathroom door clicked shut behind me, sealing me in a cocoon of false security. I avoided my reflection in the mirror as though it would confront me with truths I wasn't ready to face. My fingers trembled as I stepped out of my panties, the material sticking to my skin. Then I saw it, red smudges staining the fabric, streaking my thighs like cruel brushstrokes on a canvas. My heart pounded as I leaned forward, confirming what I already feared. Vivid splotches of blood painted my inner thighs. A wave of nausea gripped me, but I swallowed it down. My shaking hands fumbled with the faucet. The water gushed out ice-cold, but I didn't care. I stepped in without waiting for it to warm, desperate to drown the memory clinging to my skin.

The icy water hit me like a slap, but I welcomed it. Grabbing the washcloth and bar of soap, I began scrubbing forcefully, as if I could peel away the shame embedded beneath the surface. The white lather turned pink as it mixed with streaks of blood swirling down the drain. I scrubbed until my skin turned red and raw; the sting matching the turmoil inside me. Tears glided down my face, mingling with the water, silent witnesses to my breaking point.

Why did I flirt with Derrick? The question stabbed at me. Why did I go to that empty house with him? What kind of stupid girl thinks an older boy actually likes her? The blame came in waves, crashing over me, suffocating me. *This is my fault,* I thought. *I should've known better.* A fresh surge of shame bubbled up as my mind conjured the aftermath of telling anyone. No one would believe me, I realized, bitterly. They'd think I was a slut.

Blood streaked down my legs, a stark reminder of what I had lost. I cranked up the hot water and scrubbed furiously, trying to wash away this nightmare. The hot water slowly replaced the cold, but I didn't flinch. Turning the dial hotter, I hoped the scalding water would burn away the invisible filth, the memory, the guilt. My skin screamed for relief, but I refused to stop until I couldn't take it anymore.

Finally, I turned the shower off, my breath heaving, my body trembling.

I stepped out cautiously, wrapping myself tightly in a towel as though it could shield me from the world. My wet hair dripped onto my shoulders, each drop a mocking reminder of what I couldn't wash away. Hugging the towel closer, I shuffled softly to the kitchen. The dim glow of the stove clock guided me as I fumbled through the cabinet for a plastic shopping bag. The air smelled faintly of leftovers as I dug into the trash can, pushing aside scraps of dinner, paper towels, and coffee grounds until I found a deep enough spot. With shaking hands, I buried my stained panties at the bottom, pressing them down as if trying to erase their existence. The soap at the kitchen sink stung the raw patches on my hands as I scrubbed off the traces of trash and shame.

Slipping quietly into the darkened room I shared with Mama, I tiptoed toward the dresser and grabbed a pair of pajamas. The floorboards creaked faintly beneath me; the sound echoing like a warning. My hands trembled as I pulled the fabric over my weak frame, moving with the stealth of a shadow, desperate not to disturb Mama. Her soft, steady breathing reassured me she hadn't stirred. With a silent prayer, I slid under the blanket and into the warmth of her presence, careful not to jostle the bed.

Lying there, my body stiffened as the events of the day unfurled in my mind like the opening scenes of a horror movie. Each moment played in vivid detail, the dialogue, the fear, the humiliation, looping endlessly in a macabre replay. I stared into the darkness, my eyes wide and unblinking, as though afraid that closing them would make the images sharper, and the memories more real.

I turned my head slightly toward Mama, her silhouette outlined faintly by the moonlight filtering through the curtains. Desperately, I wanted to wake her, spill everything, and feel her embrace, knowing everything would be alright. The words caught in my throat, tangled in fear and shame. I lay silent, my heart racing, the pain in my chest matched only by the burning ache of helplessness.

That night, and so many nights after, I found myself in this exact position, wide awake in the darkness, haunted by memories too heavy to carry alone. The blanket cocooned me, but couldn't protect me from the dauntless storm of my thoughts. Each time I closed my eyes, the reel began again, dragging me deeper into the suffocating weight of it all.

Losing my virginity to rape shattered me physically and emotionally in ways I couldn't articulate. The offense left me hollow, as though the very essence of who I was had been taken, leaving behind only fragments. I avoided mirrors for weeks, unable to look at myself without feelings of shame and anger bubbling under my skin. Was it my fault? Should I have been stronger? The questions clawed at me, though I knew deep down that the blame belonged to him. Still, the feelings of self-doubt and violation were relentless, like a storm raging inside me. My trauma was no longer contained within the walls of my memories with Curtis. The sexual abuse and rape I endured painted my reality in dark, heavy strokes, filling my mind with two devastating lies: that the world was inherently dangerous and that my body existed solely for men's sexual satisfaction. These beliefs, though false, felt unshakably real. They whispered, there's nothing you can do to change this. So why try?

For so long, I carried those lies as though they were truths etched into my soul. They influenced every decision, every relationship, every way I perceived myself. If the world was dangerous, I figured it was safer to build walls, to shut out love and vulnerability. I detached from my body, treating it as an object rather than a part of myself, believing it was only for others. These beliefs created a self-destructive path filled with pain I couldn't avoid because I never learned my worth.

Those lies took an unimaginable amount of time to unlearn. To sit with the uncomfortable truth that what happened was not my fault, and that the experience didn't make me broken or unworthy. Healing has been a difficult and unpredictable process, full of setbacks and challenges. There were times I thought I would never feel whole again. In fact, I cannot remember a time in my childhood I ever felt whole. There were moments when the weight of shame felt too heavy to bear. But over time, through therapy, self-reflection, and the love of those who saw me for more than my trauma, I rebuilt.

Multiple therapeutic methods helped me realize that my body belongs to me, and is not something to be conquered, exploited, or used as a tool. I saw the world not only for its dangers but also for its beauty, the kindness that still existed, and the resilience within me. I found that healing didn't mean erasing the scars, but embracing them as part of my story, reminders of the battles I had survived.

To anyone reading this who feels broken, lost, or trapped by the weight of their own pain: You are not what happened to you. You are not the lies your trauma taught you. Healing is possible, even when it feels distant and unattainable. It starts with small steps, with moments of grace for yourself, and with the courage to believe that you are worthy of love, safety, and peace. Your worth is infinite, and your story is still being written. In the words of my amazing grandmother, Marilyn Santoro, "Never stop persevering!"

CHAPTER 18

A LOVE NEVER BORN

BY AGE THIRTEEN, THE concept of love, for me, was always tangled with pain, guilt, and longing. It wasn't something pure or romantic; it was a battlefield where I fought to find my worth, often losing myself in the process. My journey toward understanding love, and all the ways it had failed me, started with a decision to surrender and begin again. I sat in the back pew of the small church with a few friends who had invited me on multiple occasions. The choir's voices rose, filling the air with melodies of redemption and salvation. My pounding heart gripped me as the preacher spoke of forgiveness, and I clenched my hands tightly in my lap.

"No sin is too great," he said. "No past too shameful."

When the altar call came, my feet moved before my mind could stop them.

Kneeling there, silently sobbing, I begged Jesus for a new start. I wanted to feel saved, to feel clean, but the guilt clung to me like a second skin. No matter how many prayers I said or how many elders laid hands on me, I still felt unworthy. I left that church forgiven in theory, but feeling horrible in reality. I told myself I would be different. No boyfriends, no sex. I couldn't risk reopening the wounds left by the rape. That said, trauma is insidious: it doesn't just fade away because you want it to. It changes the way you see the world, the way you see yourself.

I tried to avoid men for about six months, but their attention was intoxicating. The way they looked at me, their compliments and charm, were the only things that made me feel seen, even if it made me feel wrong. From Curtis to Derrick, I learned to stop fighting. Somewhere deep down, I believed my only purpose was to please men, to offer whatever they wanted. After all, wasn't that what life had taught me so far? As hard as I tried to resist and live the life the Preachers talked about, I was no match for Anthony Johnson.

Minding my own business on my way to the bus stop following another afternoon at Sunrise Mall, I had no inkling of the life-altering event that awaited me. The mall parking lot played its usual soundtrack, loud rap music thundering from cars with souped-up sound systems, rims, and sometimes hydraulics. Snoop Dogg, Ice Cube, and DJ Quik were all part of the scene, and the baseline vibrations were as familiar as the neon signs glowing over the food court.

As I walked, the rumble of a car's bass approached from behind, the vibrations buzzing through my body in a way I found oddly comforting. It was routine; I didn't even look back. This time was different. Instead of the music swelling louder as the car sped past, it did the opposite: it got quieter. That made me pause. Glancing over my shoulder, curiosity tugging at me, I caught sight of the car slowing to match my pace, and then our eyes locked. Sitting in the driver's seat was a man who seemed to have stepped straight out of a Tyler Perry movie: one of the sexiest Black men I'd ever seen in my thirteen years of life. Standing out like warm amber against the backdrop of his smooth, milk-chocolate skin, his light brown eyes were captivating. Like an artist's creation, his cornrows framed his face with perfect edges. His lips were the lure, pulling me in like a moth to a flame, full, glossy, and shimmering as if the sun itself had kissed them. My heart skipped, and without hesitation, I gave him an inviting smile.

"What's up, sexy?" His voice flowed out like warm honey, smooth and captivating, with confidence that could melt ice.

I couldn't stop the grin that spread across my face.

"Hey! What's up?" I replied. My voice was higher than normal, dripping with all the flirtation I could muster.

"What's your name?" His eyes locked with mine.

I tilted my head, pouted my lips, and twisted my neck just like I'd seen grown women do in the movies. "What's yours?"

He laughed, a deep laugh that felt warm and infectious, like he was letting me in on a secret.

"Anthony. My name's Anthony. Now you."

"Christina," I replied, trying to sound coy but struggling to keep my grin in check.

"You need a ride?" he asked, flashing a smile that showcased his perfect teeth.

I hesitated, torn between the warning voice in my head and the thrill of his attention. "No, I'm okay." I glanced at the bus stop.

"You sure?" he pressed, his tone smooth.

"I'm sure." I was trying to play it cool but feeling my heart race and desperately wanting to accept the ride.

"Well then," he leaned slightly toward me, "can I get your number?"

I thought for a moment, pretending to weigh my options, and then shot back with a sly grin, "Nah. Let me get yours." He laughed again, shaking his head like my boldness impressed him.

"Alright then." He reached into his car and handed me a crumpled Foot Locker receipt with a number scribbled on it.

I took it, my fingertips brushing his for just a moment, and smiled big enough to show all my teeth. As I walked away, tucking the receipt into my pocket, I pieced together the clues. Even then, a part of me knew the pre-written number meant I wasn't special. I was just another girl. A part of me hesitated, but his smile erased my doubts like chalk from a blackboard. I was too young to realize that predators don't always come with warning signs; they often arrive wrapped in charm. Still, I couldn't stop the thrill coursing through me. In my naive, thirteen-year-old mind, Anthony was a jackpot, a sexy twenty-two-year-old man with a car and presumably enough money to drop $80 on Nikes. Though part of me suspected it might not even be his receipt, I didn't care. I was smitten, caught up in the fantasy of what I thought his attention meant.

That evening, I couldn't wait any longer. I had to call him. The romance movies always said to play it cool, but I barely made it a few hours before giving in. When Anthony answered, he immediately asked when he could take me out, and my excitement soared. Sadly, I couldn't go out until the weekend because of school, and I spent the week calling him daily, hoping to hear his voice.

Each time, his mother picked up and dismissed me with a sharp, "He ain't here," hanging up before I could respond.

By Friday, I had nearly given up hope, until the phone rang. "I'll get it!" I shouted, leaping from the couch before Mama could intercept the call. It was Anthony. My insides fluttered with butterflies as we exchanged quick pleasantries.

Within seconds, he asked, "Can I pick you up tonight?"

"Yes!" I said without hesitation. "But you'll have to meet me at the corner store parking lot."

Without asking Mama for permission, I told her I was spending the night at my friend Sierra's house and taking the bus there. She nodded, none the wiser, and gave me the go-ahead. Within thirty minutes, I was ready and waiting at the corner store, my heart racing as I spotted his car pulling up just as I arrived.

I couldn't help but let my mind wander to all the possibilities for the night. Where would Anthony take me? Would I end up meeting his mama? Maybe we'd go to a nice restaurant or catch a movie at Birdcage Walk, the dollar theater where I spent so many weekends imagining a life like the ones on-screen. Whatever adventures awaited; I was sure they'd be amazing. When Anthony's maroon Cutlass pulled up, I felt a flutter of excitement. Leaning over, he unlocked the passenger door. I hopped in eagerly, my nerves barely holding me together, as the leather seats burned the backs of my thighs.

"Can I get a hug?" he asked. His voice was like velvet dipped in honey, rich and effortless, wrapping around me with undeniable charm.

Ignoring the burning sensation, I scooted closer and wrapped my arms around him, my heart racing. Before I could move back to the passenger side, he leaned in and kissed me on the cheek. Instinctively, I turned my face toward his, and suddenly, we were sharing my first real intimate kiss. It was like a scene from one of those romance movies I loved, sweet, magical, and for a moment, it pushed the weight of my past to the side.

"Where are we going?" I asked, trying not to sound too giddy.

"To my boy's house," he replied casually, like it was the most obvious thing in the world.

As I scooted back to the passenger seat, his hand gently touched my thigh.

"Nah, sit next to me," he said with a smile that made my knees weak.

Without hesitation, I slid back over and fumbled around for the middle seatbelt. "Uh, where's the seatbelt?" I asked, trying to act nonchalant.

"Ain't got one," Anthony said, shrugging, like it was no big deal. Caught between my sense of safety and the allure of romance, I paused for a split second. Naturally I chose romance, and spent the twenty-minute drive snuggling up to him, feeling like I was in a dream.

I tried to make conversation, but the loud rap music pouring out of his speakers crackled with bass, drowning out my efforts. Instead, I let myself sink into the moment, stealing glances at him as the scent of his Cool Water cologne clung to the air, thick and heavy. The scent of crisp ocean air mixed with warm musk made him seem like the very definition of untamed confidence, and I leaned in closer just to breathe it in. When we pulled into a rundown apartment complex in Del Paso Heights, I couldn't help but laugh. *This is definitely not a house,* I thought, the internal voice in my head screaming, *Oh hell no, this place looks sketchy! Tell him to take you home right now.* Instead of listening to that inner voice, I ignored it and let Anthony help me out of the driver's side door, feeling a thrill at the touch of his hand. As we climbed the steps, the familiar scent of weed hit me like a brick. Though I had never smoked it, I knew the funky stench well enough. The hallway reeked of it, and it wasn't hard to tell which apartment was to blame as we arrived at his boy's house.

Inside, the air was stale, thick with weed smoke and the sour tang of unwashed bodies. Something inside me shivered. This wasn't the romantic getaway I'd hoped for. It felt like a trap disguised as a hangout. Anthony introduced me to his friends, Marcus and Tyson. Neither one looked up from their intense game of Mortal Kombat, only nodding in unison before resuming their mission to destroy each other on-screen. Standing behind the couch, I couldn't help but get drawn into the action of the combating characters. Sub-Zero hurled an icy projectile while Scorpion shouted, "Get over here!" and retaliated with his iconic spear. The sound of punches and kicks filled the room as the players barked at each other.

"Dang!" I murmured under my breath, a grin tugging at the corners of my lips.

For a second, I wanted nothing more than to grab a controller and show them what I could do, even though I was bad at the game.

Anthony's warm hand wrapped around mine, pulling me back to the present. "I didn't bring you here to play video games," he said with a teasing smile, reminding me why I was there.

Reluctantly, I let him lead me away, my eyes lingering on the screen for just a moment longer. As much as I hated to admit it, I was more intrigued by Mortal Kombat than I should have been, but Anthony's charm recaptured my attention.

He guided me around the corner to the first bedroom, his hand lightly resting on the small of my back. Each step felt heavier than the last as my gut screamed louder this time, a warning I couldn't ignore. *He's going to want more than just making out,* the inner voice warned, but I swallowed the lump in my throat and kept moving, ignoring the voice of reason once again.

The room was dimly lit and un-kept, a space that instantly made my skin crawl. The air was heavy, filled with the stale scent of sweat and something faintly sweet, like old cologne. Clothes lay scattered on the floor, and in the middle of the mess sat a single mattress on the ground, poorly serving as a bed. The room was thick with the stench of stale sweat and unwashed sheets, a funky, suffocating odor that clung to the air like a bad memory. I hesitated at the doorway, every part of me wanting to turn and leave, but Anthony's presence pulled me forward.

"Come on, sit down," he said, his voice mellow and inviting, as if the room's state didn't matter.

I perched on the edge of the mattress, my legs feeling shaky as I glanced around, searching for anything that could distract me from the growing sense of unease. Anthony climbed to the top of the mattress, leaning back against the wall with an effortless confidence. He motioned for me to join him, patting the spot beside him with a small smile. My brain whispered, *This isn't right. You're not ready. You don't even know him.* But louder than that was the fear that if I said no, he'd leave. Being left alone felt worse than being touched. I hesitated for a moment, my gut twisting in protest, but I pushed it aside. Maybe this could still be the special night I'd imagined, I told myself, even as doubt showered down on me. I crawled up to sit beside him, the mattress creaking beneath our weight.

What started as shy kisses quickly turned into something more. His hands roamed, his touch insistent, and before I realized it, our clothes were on the floor beside the tangled sheets. My born-again virginity, the promise I had made to myself and God to wait until I was married, was freely given to Anthony. In my mind, he was someone special, someone who could change my life forever. But I was as wrong as I was right. Anthony changed my life forever, just not in the way I hoped.

The encounter wasn't romantic or magical. The rush, awkwardness, and sense of inevitability made me feel hollow. As the musk in the room clung to me and the clarity of what had just happened sank in, I knew I made a mistake. The weight of it would follow me, haunting me in ways I couldn't yet comprehend. What I thought would be a defining moment of connection and love instead became a lesson in regret, a decision that would echo through the rest of my life.

Afterward, I had Anthony drop me off at the corner near Sierra's house, a place where I was always welcome, no questions asked. As his car disappeared down the street, a strange mix of relief and regret washed over me. I lingered outside for a moment, breathing in the cool night air, trying to steady myself before walking up to the door. Sierra let me in with a smile, yet I barely managed a weak one in return. She and her boyfriend disappeared into her room, leaving me alone in the living room. I tossed my bag onto the floor and made my way to the bathroom, desperate for a shower.

Standing under the stream of hot water, I scrubbed my skin until it turned red, my hands trembling as I tried to wash away the lingering scent of musk and regret again. The feelings clung to me; disappointment, shame, and the ache of a night that had gone so differently from the way I'd hoped.

Days turned into nights, and there were no calls from Anthony. Despite my frequent attempts to reach out, the silence on his end said everything I needed to hear. He had gotten what he wanted and was finished with me. I replayed our conversations over and over in my head. Did I say something wrong? Was I not enough? I didn't have the language for it then, but what I was feeling wasn't heartbreak, it was the shame of being groomed and discarded. The realization was a bitter pill to swallow, but eventually, I got the hint and stopped dialing his number; the rejection settling into a dull ache I couldn't shake. He was twenty-two. I was thirteen. It should have been criminal. It was. I thought it might be love. Now I know better. It was grooming and exploitation. It was abuse.

Weeks passed, and life carried on, but I couldn't ignore the nagging feeling that something wasn't right. My body felt different, as though it was trying to tell me a secret I wasn't ready to hear. Deep down, I already suspected what was happening, but I pushed it aside, clinging to the hope that maybe I was wrong.

No longer able to shake this feeling, I knew I had to tell Mama. The silence in the room felt heavier than the words I was about to say. I glanced at Mama; her face was already lined with worry as she flipped through the bills scattered across the kitchen table. I opened my mouth, but nothing came out at first. My heart raced, my palms damp with sweat. Finally, I forced the words out in a rush, afraid I might choke on them if I hesitated.

"I think I need to go to the doctor. I missed my period."

Her hand froze midair, the envelope she held slipping from her fingers. She stared at me, her expression a mix of disbelief and dread.

"What did you just say, Tina?"

"I'm late," I whispered, unable to meet her eyes. "I've been late for weeks."

The rest of the day passed in a blur. Mom didn't yell or cry, but the tightness in her voice as she made the doctor's appointment spoke volumes.

Sitting in that cold, sterile room, I clung to a shred of hope. Hope that this was all a mistake, that my body was just playing tricks on me. When the doctor walked in, the look on his face said it all.

"You're pregnant," he confirmed, his voice clinical and detached.

The words echoed in my head, drowning out everything else. I had known deep down but, hearing it aloud was like being hit by a freight train.

At first, I was terrified. How could I be a mother? I was just a kid myself. In the quiet moments when I let my mind wander, a strange excitement crept in. I imagined holding a tiny baby in my arms, loving them the way I always longed to be loved. Maybe, just maybe, this was my chance to create a family of my own, a family where love wasn't conditional, where safety was given. Reality, however, wasn't so kind. I had no job, no money, and no plan. But in my delusion, I convinced myself it would all work out. Somehow, I'd figure it out.

The first blow came in the days after I found out I was pregnant. I called Anthony over and over, desperate to tell him, to hear something, anything, that resembled support. Each time his mom answered, her voice was curt and dismissive.

"He ain't here," she'd say before hanging up, the dial tone ringing in my ears like a cruel punctuation.

For a week, I tried, hoping that one of those calls would end differently. Finally, in frustration, I blurted,

"Can you just tell him Christina is pregnant?" before she could hang up again.

Minutes later, my phone rang, and there he was, his voice cold and sharp. He didn't offer congratulations or concerns, just accusations.

"I don't think it's mine," he said flatly. "You need to take care of it. Stop calling me."

His words felt like a slap, and as the line went dead, the weight of his rejection crushed any small hope to which I'd been clinging. He had revealed himself as nothing more than an irresponsible coward, yet somehow, I still turned his rejection inward, believing the fault lay with me.

The second and final blow came with my parents' rejection. The call to my dad was one I had been dreading but knew I had to make. My hands trembled as I picked up the phone, dialing his number with a mix of hope and desperation.

"Hi Priscilla, can I talk to Darius?" I asked when my stepmother answered, trying to sound calm.

Her soft voice replied, "Hold on, honey. I'll get him." I waited, my heart pounding in my chest.

A moment later, his familiar voice came through the line, light and joyful, like nothing in the world could shake him.

"What's going on, ham hock?"

The nickname made me cringe. I hated it, always had, but I could never bring myself to tell him. This wasn't the time to correct him, anyway.

"I need your help," I started hesitantly, the words shaky as they left my mouth. Before he could say anything, I blurted it out, unable to hold it in any longer. "I'm pregnant, and my mom says I can't stay with her if I keep the baby. Can I come live with you?"

The silence that followed was deafening. It stretched on so long that I wondered if the line had gone dead. My chest tightened, and I pressed the phone closer to my ear.

"Are you there?" I mumbled, my voice barely a whisper.

"I'm here," he finally said, his voice distant. "But you're not coming to live with me just because you got yourself pregnant."

His words hit like a punch to the throat, and his indifferent tone, final, left no room for argument, no room for hope. Feeling the air leave my lungs, tears welled in my eyes.

"I have nowhere else to go." I stammered, the words foreign and heavy on my tongue.

He didn't waver. "That's not my problem," he replied bluntly. "You made this choice, and now you have to deal with it."

I bit my lip, trying to stop the sobs that were threatening to spill out. "Okay," I whispered, my voice breaking. "I get it."

"Take care of yourself Christina," he said, as though those words would somehow soften the blow.

The line went dead, and I sat there, the phone still pressed to my ear, stunned by the weight of his rejection. I had called him for support, for safety, for a lifeline. Instead, he had cut the last thread to which I had been clinging, leaving me to drown in my desperation. The hurt was indescribable; a deep cut that would take many seasons to heal.

The rejection from my parents was a wound I thought couldn't hurt any deeper. My mom's ultimatum to leave if I kept the baby and my dad's cold refusal to let me live with him left me reeling, unsure of where to turn. It was Anthony's rejection that shattered whatever fragile pieces I had left. The way he dismissed me, denied responsibility, and told me to "take care of it" cut straight through me. His words confirmed what I was terrified of admitting: that I was truly alone. I felt like everyone had abandoned me. My parents, the people who were supposed to love me unconditionally, turned their backs when I needed them most. Anthony, who I naively believed might at least care enough to stand by me, made it clear I was nothing more than a burden to him. It was as though the walls of my world had crumbled, leaving me falling, with no one to catch me. To make matters worse, not long after my decision to have an abortion, both of my parents delivered their versions of what felt like too-late reassurances, passive admissions that pierced deeper than they realized.

My mother looked at me one day and said softly, "You know I wouldn't have kicked you out."

A few months later, during a visit to my father's house, he told me casually, "You know I would've let you come live with me."

Their words didn't offer comfort. They landed like daggers, reopening wounds I was barely managing to close. In those moments, I felt an overwhelming mix of betrayal, confusion, and rage. Why hadn't they said these things when it mattered? When I needed safety? When I needed them? Their hindsight felt like a cruel joke, as if I was supposed to have known something they never actually said.

The resentment I carried after those conversations ran deep and lingered for years. Although we shared a handful of authentic moments in the years that followed, my relationship with both of them remained strained. I was angry that they hadn't stood by me when I needed them most, and hurt that they later acted as though the door had always been open. Healing wasn't instant. It came slowly, through reflection, therapy, and time. Eventually, I saw them not just as parents, but as flawed human beings, doing the best they could with what they had. And in that understanding, I found space for forgiveness. It didn't erase the pain, but it helped me release the burden of it. The loneliness was suffocating. I had no safety net, no shoulder to cry on, no one to tell me it would be okay. I was just a scared, pregnant thirteen-year-old, backed into a corner with nowhere to go, carrying a pain I didn't know how to survive.

My mind often traveled to the moment I gave in to what I thought I had to do. The mental anguish of having an abortion at thirteen was something no one could have prepared for. In the car on the way to the abortion clinic, Mama and I sat in silence, lost in our own thoughts. In the clinical procedure room, I felt like I was outside my body, watching a nightmare unfold. My hands shook, my chest felt tight, and my heart pounded with a mix of fear, guilt, and overwhelming sadness. I didn't want to be there, but I didn't see any other choice. Everyone around me, my parents, Anthony, even the clinic staff, spoke about it like it was a simple decision, a necessary step. For me, however, it felt like I was ripping a piece of myself away, one I would never get back.

After it was over, the real torment began. I couldn't stop thinking about the what ifs. What if I had been older, stronger, or more capable? What if I had found the courage to fight for that tiny life inside me? The visions of the baby I would never hold haunted me, little fingers curling around mine, a laugh I'd never hear, a bond I'd never get to share. It was all gone, and the emptiness left behind was unbearable. I tried to convince myself it was the right decision, that I was too young and too unprepared, but those words felt hollow against the crushing weight of guilt. I hated myself for not being better, for not finding a way. At night, I'd lie awake in bed, replaying everything in my mind, feeling like I deserved the pain. I felt like a failure, not just as a girl who had made a mistake, but as a mother who had lost her chance to protect her child.

The isolation made it worse. I couldn't talk to anyone about how I felt; the shame was too heavy, and I didn't think anyone would understand. Instead, I carried the pain alone, a secret burden that felt too big for my youthful body to bear. The decision might have been the right one, but the scars it left on my heart and mind would never heal.

It took almost ten years for me to admit to anyone, even myself, that I had an abortion. For years, I told people I'd had a miscarriage. It was easier, less shameful, and I thought it would protect me from the judgment I couldn't bear to face. I even told doctors the same story during exams, layering lie upon lie, burying the truth under a thick shell of guilt and self-loathing. The shame consumed me, a constant reminder of what I had done and what I believed it said about me. All I had ever wanted was to be a mother. Even at thirteen, when I was terrified and completely ill-prepared, the idea of having someone to love unconditionally had been a small, glimmering hope in the darkness of my life. But in that tiny sterile clinic, I gave up what I saw as my one chance at that dream. No matter how much I told myself I was too young, too lost, or too unsupported to raise a child, I couldn't shake the feeling that I had failed, that I had given up something precious, something irreplaceable.

Adding insult to injury, when I joined the military at eighteen, a series of medical appointments revealed something I hadn't expected. During an exam, the doctor casually mentioned an irregular amount of scar tissue inside me. His tone was clinical, detached, as he explained it might make it difficult, if not impossible, for me to bear children in the future. The words hit me like a punch to the throat, stealing my very breath. It was as if God Himself had reached out to punish me for the decision I had made as a scared, desperate child. My dream of one day holding a baby and creating the family I longed for vanished. I had given up my chance, and now there might never be another.

The weight of that realization crushed me, compounding the shame and guilt I had carried for years. I couldn't talk about it, not even to myself. Instead, I locked it away, buried it under layers of denial and silence. The decision, and its consequences, haunted me. It was there in the quiet moments, in the ache I felt when I saw mothers with their children, in the questions I couldn't answer about my past. It shaped the way I saw myself, not as someone who had made a difficult choice, but as someone unworthy of the love and connection I had always craved. The scars weren't just physical; they were emotional, etched into my soul, a reminder of a moment that would follow me for the rest of my life. It took quite a bit of time before I could finally speak the truth, and even then, the weight of that decision lingered, a shadow I could never quite escape.

Eventually, I found the courage to face the truth I buried for so long. Slowly, I allowed myself to acknowledge what happened, not with shame, but with the honesty and compassion I had denied myself for years. I opened up to those I trusted, those I deemed worthy of knowing my deepest secret. Sharing my story wasn't easy, but it was liberating. For the first time, the weight of my guilt started to lift. Forgiveness was something I realized I deserved, not only for others, but also for myself. I slowly learned how to show myself compassion, to see that scared thirteen-year-old girl for what she was, just a child, overwhelmed and desperate, making the best choice she could in an impossible situation. I forgave her, and in doing so, I forgave myself. It took time, but I came to accept that my path might not include bearing children of my own. I allowed myself to dream of other possibilities: adoption, stepchildren, or perhaps a life where I would nurture in other ways.

Just as I had made peace with this reality, life threw me an unexpected twist. At age twenty-one, while stationed in Bad Kreuznach,

Germany, I sat in a doctor's office, complaining about fatigue, dizziness, and headaches. It had been a busy day; I'd aced a physical fitness test that morning and won the Soldier of the Month competition all before lunch. I thought I was simply dehydrated or overtired. When the doctor left to run some tests, I thought nothing of it. When she returned, her expression caught me off guard. There was a mix of apprehension and confusion on her face that made my heart skip a beat.

"Are you trying to get pregnant?" she asked cautiously.

I chuckled, shaking my head. "No. The doctors told me last year I couldn't have children because of scarring."

Her eyebrows lifted in surprise. "Well..." Pausing for a moment as though she were piecing it together herself, "It looks like that may have been hypothetical because you're definitely pregnant."

I stared at her, speechless. The words hung in the air, almost unreal. Pregnant? It didn't seem possible. My mind raced, trying to reconcile what I was hearing with everything I had believed for so long.

"Pregnant?" I finally whispered.

She nodded, a small smile playing at the corners of her lips. "Yes. You're pregnant."

I didn't know whether to laugh, cry, or collapse right there in the office. A tidal wave of emotions crashed over me, shock, disbelief, joy, and fear, all at once. I had spent over a year grieving the loss of something I thought I could never have. Now, against all odds, here it was, handed back to me in the most unexpected way.

Tears began streaming down my face, and within seconds, uncontrollable sobs consumed me. It wasn't just crying; it was a raw, ugly release of emotions that left me gasping for air, the words stumbling out in fragmented, inaudible phrases between heaving breaths. My body trembled as years of pain, guilt, and disbelief seemed to surge to the surface all at once.

The doctor, her expression softening with concern, hesitated. She must have thought this wasn't good news.

Gently, she spoke. "You have options..."

"No!" I gasped, my voice sharp and trembling, cutting her off mid-sentence. "I will never do that again!"

She blinked, clearly startled by the force of my reaction, and took a step back, as though recalibrating.

After a moment, her voice softened further. "How are you feeling?"

I wiped at my tear-soaked face, trying to find enough clarity to answer. "I... I had an abortion when I was thirteen," I said, the words heavy and deliberate. My voice cracked as I continued, "And when I joined the Army, I was told I wouldn't be able to have children. And now..." I paused, struggling to steady my breathing as I looked at her. "Now you're telling me I'm pregnant?"

The room seemed to still, her face a mix of understanding and quiet compassion.

"I'm just in shock," I admitted, my voice barely above a whisper.

I sat there, my mind spinning, trying to process the enormity of what I'd just been told. After everything, the pain of that decision at thirteen, the years of guilt and regret, the acceptance of what I thought was my fate, this moment felt like a miracle.

I placed my hands on my stomach, barely able to believe that life was growing inside me. My body, once dismissed as broken and scarred, was now creating something extraordinary. I was going to be a mother. It felt as though the heavens had reached out, offering me a gift I thought I would never receive. And in that moment, amidst the tears and disbelief, I made a silent promise to myself and to the baby growing within me: I would cherish this gift with every ounce of my being. This time, I would do everything I could to be the mother I had always dreamed of being.

Although it wasn't the path I had envisioned, I was thrilled and deeply grateful for the opportunity to become a mother. It felt like a second chance, a gift I never expected to receive. But even with the joy of this new chapter, a part of me always has and always will mourn My Love Never Born, the child I let go of at thirteen. Over time, I've come to believe that the decision I made as a scared, overwhelmed girl was the right one for me at that moment in my life. As painful as it was, it paved the way for me to grow, heal, and ultimately, to become the mother I needed to be, not just for the beautiful baby boy I was about to bring into the world, but also for the two sons who would follow in the years to come.

That choice, as harrowing and life-altering as it was, became the bridge to a future I couldn't see. It allowed me, when the time was finally right, to step into motherhood with open arms and a heart ready to pour out everything I had longed for as a child. It gave me the chance to try, to truly try, to give my children what I never had: unconditional love, stability, and the unwavering presence of a parent who, though still healing from deep childhood wounds, was determined to be the best mother I could be.

The pain of aborting my first child still lingers, like a shadow that softens but never fully disappears. Yet, it stands as a testament to the strength I discovered within myself, to the resilience that carried me through the darkest of times and led me here. My children became more than just my family; they became my purpose, the light that guided me toward redemption. They are my greatest joy, the embodiment of love and hope, and the reason I know that even from the most broken places, beauty can emerge.

CHAPTER 19

JOURNEY THROUGH MOURNING

THEY SAY DEATH COMES in threes, a grim, unspoken rule whispered among those left behind. When Rebecca Hayes died, it felt like the first crack splitting through the fragile foundation of my world. Rebecca wasn't just my preschool babysitter; she was a fixture of warmth and care, one whose presence lingered long after our families moved in different directions. She had a way of making me feel seen, of taking up space in my heart so effortlessly that I didn't realize how much of it she filled, until the space was gone. The news came early one morning before school, delivered by my mom in a voice so soft it was almost a whisper.

Her words felt too big to say out loud, but too urgent to keep inside. "Tina, Rebecca Hayes passed away."

For a moment, I just stared at her, dumbfounded, as though the words hadn't registered, as if they were floating in the air between us, too surreal to grasp. Rebecca Hayes. Passed. The two concepts didn't belong in the same sentence, not in my mind, not in my life. It was like the universe had made a mistake; one it couldn't possibly take back. The weight of her words pressed down on me, but my mind rebelled, clinging to disbelief.

"What do you mean?" I finally asked, hoping there was some mistake, some misunderstanding.

The look in my mother's eyes confirmed what I already knew deep down. This was real, and she was gone. Rebecca, the woman who filled every room with her sharp wit and louder laugh, who could make even the most unhappy toddler smile with glee, the woman who had spent hours upon hours teaching me the most mundane preschool tasks, was gone. My mom's timing was awful, but timing with death usually is.

"Her funeral has already happened," Mama added. That part hit me harder. I hadn't even known she was sick. It had been a considerable amount of time, in fact years, since we had last laid eyes on her. Busy schedules and endless to-do lists had overtaken us, and our annual visits became a distant memory, a forgotten ritual. No closure, no goodbye, just the knowledge that she was gone. It felt unreal. My emotions finally catching up released in a stream of tears, hot and unrelenting, streaking down my face as a knot tightened in my chest. Rebecca's laughter, her smile, her hugs felt like they could shield me from the world. The events felt impossibly distant now, as if something had ripped them from my grasp.

"I'm sorry," Mama added, her voice breaking slightly, but the words offered no comfort. They weren't enough to fill the gaping hole that had just opened in my heart. I wanted to scream, to cry louder, to ask why this had happened, but I couldn't find the strength. Instead, I sat there, the grief settling over me like a heavy, suffocating blanket.

School felt like a distant, absurd thought, but I went anyway, carrying the weight of her absence with me. The day passed in a blur, the noise of the hallways and classrooms muffled under the deafening silence inside my head. Rebecca Hayes was gone, and with her, a piece of my life as I knew it.

My next devastation came by phone. I got a call about Shannon Rae. She wasn't blood-related, but she was family in every way that mattered. She was our no-nonsense, foul-mouthed, chain-smoking force to be reckoned with: an amazing neighbor. A woman who didn't just tell it like it was, she told it with a cigarette dangling from her lips and enough sass to stop you in your tracks. Shannon Rae had gossip on everyone but always backed it up with the biggest heart. If you needed a place to stay, she'd find a room. If you needed a meal, she'd find food, and if you needed a reality check, she'd give it to you without skipping a beat. When I heard she had gone to the hospital for pneumonia, I thought little of it. Shannon Rae was tough as nails; pneumonia didn't stand a chance against her, or so I thought. Within a couple of days, she was gone, and just like that, the neighborhood lost its anchor.

Her funeral was the opposite of Rebecca's quiet absence. Family, neighbors, and countless others who knew Shannon Rae packed the funeral home. My Aunt Miranda, Shannon Rae's daughter Tammy, our friend Jasmine, and I sat together in the front row, all dressed in black, trying to look respectable. The funeral director started in a somber tone, and it took no time at all for us to dissolve into laughter.

We were not trying to be disrespectful, but Shannon Rae would've hated a stuffy, overly serious event. She would've wanted us to remember her as she was: bold, hilarious, and unapologetically herself.

We whispered stories back and forth, trying to stifle our giggles but failing miserably.

"Remember that time Shannon Rae sent us chasing the mailman down the street for delivering her neighbor's package to the wrong house?" Jasmine whispered, barely able to get the words out before bursting into laughter.

"And the time she made us tear the living room apart searching for her pack of cigarettes that she swore were there that morning. Come to find out she had smoked them all and threw the pack away. The look on her face when she pulled the empty pack out of the trash was priceless and we all fell out laughing," Tammy added, wiping tears from her eyes.

My Aunt Miranda leaned in, her voice low but dripping with mischief. "What about that time she told that nosy neighbor, Mr. Thompson, that if he kept peeking through her blinds every time he walked by, she'd moon him?"

The memory came flooding back, and we couldn't help but laugh. Mr. Thompson had been peeking through the blinds again while walking his scruffy brown mutt, and Shannon Rae had had enough. "That's it!" she declared, storming across the room. She yanked the blinds open with one hand, her other holding the edge of her housecoat. "You want a real show? You're about to get one!"

We all froze in shock as she reached for the hem of her housecoat and began lifting it higher and higher. The room went completely still, our eyes wide as we held our breath. Just as the fabric began to reach an indecent height, she dropped it back down and spun around to face us with a smirk.

"You all really thought I was going to do it, didn't you? And you were just going to let me!"

The stunned silence broke, and we erupted into laughter, doubling over as the absurdity of it hit us.

"Mom!" Tammy howled. "We didn't know if you were serious!"

Grinning from ear to ear, Shannon Rae shrugged. "Just wanted to make sure you were paying attention. Now, somebody close those damn blinds!"

It was such a classic Shannon Rae moment, bold, unpredictable, and hilarious. Even now, retelling it made the laughter spill out all over again, her spirit alive in every detail of the story.

With tears dripping down our faces, a mix of hysterical laughter and the ache of losing her, we honored Shannon Rae the only way we knew how. It felt so wrong and so right at the same time. Laughter is healing, they say, and in that moment, it was the only way to make sense of the loss. Shannon Rae was larger than life and trying to mourn her with silence and solemnity would've been a disservice to her memory. As the laughter faded, the ache remained, her absence settling in like a shadow over everything she had touched. The neighborhood seemed quieter, duller, as if the spark she brought to it had been extinguished. I tried to find comfort in the thought that she would have wanted us to carry on with the same boldness she lived her life, but the weight of her loss lingered.

Then, before I could fully catch my breath, my Great Aunt Cynthia passed. I thought the "threes" were complete, but each loss felt unique, its pain distinct and sharp. Aunt Cynthia was the gentlest spirit you could ever meet, kind, loving, and with a presence that felt almost sacred. She wasn't just family; she was a source of warmth and calm, someone whose quiet strength could ease even the stormiest of hearts. To me, she was an angel, a constant reminder that kindness could shape the world in its own quiet way.

Her life was full of simple joys, the greatest of which was her love for sewing and crocheting. Aunt Cynthia's hands were rarely idle; they were always busy creating something beautiful, stitching love and care into every quilt, every blanket, every piece she made. Her quilts were works of art, pieced together with precision and devotion, and her crocheted blankets carried the comfort only something handmade with love could provide. One of her blankets became a cherished heirloom in my family. She had crocheted it for me when I was a baby, a soft, intricate masterpiece that I was wrapped in the moment I came into the world. Years later, I passed the same blanket on to my own children, wrapping them in the love Aunt Cynthia had woven into every stitch. It wasn't just a blanket; it was a tradition, a symbol of her care that spanned generations.

Before she passed, I had the chance to visit her at my Aunt Susan's ranch, where she was being cared for by her sisters in her final days. The ranch was peaceful, its rolling hills and wide-open sky offering a sense of calm that felt fitting for Aunt Cynthia. Upon entering, I noticed how frail she looked, her hands still and resting upon the quilt. Her eyes still held their familiar sparkle, and her smile, though soft, was as warm as ever.

I sat beside her, struggling to find the words to express everything I felt. My voice trembling, all I could say was, "I love you."

Her smile deepened, and she reached for my hand, barely able to grip. Leaving her that day was one of the hardest things I've ever done. I lingered in the doorway, taking one last look at her, trying to memorize the warmth in her eyes and the serenity in her smile. As I turned to leave, I felt an indescribable ache followed by a deep gratitude for the time we'd shared and the chance to tell her I loved her. When the call came that she had passed, I felt the loss deeply. Aunt Cynthia's absence was profound, her gentle spirit leaving a quiet void that nothing could replace. Her legacy remained, stitched into every quilt she made, every blanket she crocheted, every memory she left behind.

Under the cover of night came the fourth. Thomas Prescott wasn't blood, but he might as well have been. He had been Mama's friend from our old apartment complex. Though if I'm honest, I was never quite sure if he was just a friend or something more. What I knew was how his presence changed the energy in our home. When Thomas was around, Mama smiled more. She laughed in a way that felt real, like it came from somewhere deep, not the tired, polite chuckles I was used to seeing.

Thomas had a quiet strength about him. He didn't raise his voice or demand attention, but somehow, everyone noticed him anyway. His calming presence made you feel safe just by being in the room. He listened and was genuinely interested in what I had to say, and that alone made him rare.

While we lived in that complex, he was a steady fixture in our lives, showing up when things were hard and staying long after others disappeared. He'd help Mama carry groceries or fix little things around the apartment, but it was more than that. He saw her. He saw us. And without saying much, he made me feel like we mattered.

When we moved away, we lost touch. Life swept us in different directions, and the chaos that followed left little room for staying connected. But Thomas? He never left my heart. Even years later, his name still held weight, tucked into a soft place inside me. The kind of place you reserve for someone who once made the world feel just a little bit lighter.

His art stood out most to me. Drawings filled with intricate details that made me want to look closer, to study the lines and layers. I still had some of his pieces tucked away in a folder under my bed, treasures from a time when life felt a little more bearable. He had given them to me in moments of kindness, handing them over with a quiet smile that seemed to say, I see you. Those drawings were more than just pictures. They were memories, connections, proof that someone had taken the time to create something beautiful and share it with me. I hadn't seen him in years. Life had pulled us apart, as it so often does, but I always thought of him fondly. So when the news came, it hit like a sucker punch to the jaw. This was the fourth devastating loss I'd faced in high school. However, this loss was significantly different.

Thomas had taken his own life. He shot himself by the river, just a short walk from the apartment complex where we currently lived. The news came without warning, without ceremony. No funeral, no gathering to remember him, no space to grieve together. Just a sudden, brutal void where he used to be.

This loss carried a different sting. It wasn't like the others, where laughter and shared memories could soften the edges of grief. Thomas' death left a wound that felt sharper, deeper, and more personal. There was no way to wrap it in humor, no stories to tell that would make it hurt less. Instead, there was just the overwhelming question of why.

I replayed the brief moments in my head, trying to find a sign, something that would make sense of it all. The way he used to sit at our kitchen table, sketching while Mama talked. The quiet conversations we'd have when he handed me a new drawing, asking what I saw in it, as though my opinion mattered. His calm presence had always seemed unshakable, like the world's chaos couldn't touch him. It had, though.

Imagining how someone so talented, so kind, could reach a place of such despair shook me to my core. I couldn't stop thinking about how alone he must have felt in those last moments, how much pain he must have been carrying. Then the guilt came, creeping in like a shadow. Had I missed something? Could I have said or done anything that would have made a difference?

Thomas' death opened a door I'd tried to ignore for years, one marked "Suicide." Before that, it was like a shadow at the edge of my vision, always there but never in focus. His death blasted that door wide open, stripped its hinges, porch light, and everything that held it shut. Where the once dim porch light flickered, a new, flashing neon arrow boldly stood, beckoning me forward every time life felt too heavy to bear. The sign glowed brightest during turbulence, especially in those moments when the storm inside me reached hurricane levels. It hummed softly, soothing, and tempting, even when the world outside thought I was thriving.

My laughter, my humor, and my ability to light up a room were my shields, carefully constructed to keep even the most observant from seeing the cracks underneath. I did, however, see that doorway. Countless times, I leaned against its frame, finding brief moments of solace in the idea of escape. I stood there, staring into the dark, imagining the peace it promised. I even tried to step through it three times. Each attempt left me feeling more broken than before, my failure only confirming what I already believed about myself: that I was incapable, even at ending my pain.

Over time, I boarded up that doorway, one fragile layer at a time. At first, it was cheap plywood riddled with holes, the light still leaking through, flickering just enough to catch my attention. Eventually, a team of carpenters and electricians came. Countless doctors, therapists, mentors, close family and friends who saw the darkness I tried so hard to hide taught me how to reinforce those boards, layer by layer, until the light grew dimmer. They taught me how to rewire the neon sign, dismantling its power bit by bit, and replacing its hum with fresh voices of love, faith and hope. It wasn't a straightforward process. My impatient heart often demanded the installation of a steel door with locks and hinges so strong I could never open it again, no matter how tempted I might be. Sadly, that's not how healing works.

My healing journey has comprised multiple therapeutic approaches, each contributing a unique piece to my recovery. One of the most transformative has been Cognitive Behavioral Therapy (CBT), an evidence-based approach that helped me identify and challenge the deeply rooted negative thoughts that shaped how I saw myself and the world around me. With time, I understood that many of the beliefs I carried about my worth, safety, and ability to be loved weren't facts, but survival strategies developed in response to trauma. By learning to challenge those thoughts, I slowly rebuilt my self-worth and confidence.

There were seasons when the weight of my past felt unbearable, and I needed more support than talk therapy alone could provide. I've explored medication as a tool in my healing process, not as a cure, but as a bridge. For me, trying medication wasn't about erasing emotions; it was about creating enough mental stability and clarity to do the deeper healing work. It wasn't always easy. Finding the right fit took time, and so did releasing the shame I'd internalized about needing extra help. But I've learned that there's no shame in doing what's necessary to care for your mental health. Healing is not one-size-fits-all.

There were times when the burden of my trauma became too heavy to carry alone, and I entered inpatient treatment. Those were some of the hardest yet most necessary chapters of my life, where healing meant stripping everything back to the rawest version of myself. In those quiet, clinical rooms, I found space to pause, reflect, and breathe. Outpatient therapy followed, offering consistency and support as I reentered the world, carrying new tools and insights with me.

I also found significant benefits in mindfulness practices, learning to sit with my emotions rather than run from them. Through guided meditation, breath work, and grounding techniques, I discovered that peace could exist in the present moment, even if only for a few minutes at a time. That sense of presence became a lifeline in moments when the past threatened to consume me.

Over time, I explored other modalities, including inner child work, journaling, trauma-informed yoga, and group therapy, each offering new layers of understanding and healing. Some worked better than others at different points in my journey, and I've come to learn that healing is not linear. There is no one-size-fits-all. What helped most was allowing myself to remain open, to keep trying, keep learning, and keep showing up, even on the days when all I wanted was to give up.

Grief and pain have a way of teaching us what we're made of, even when it feels like it's breaking us. My battle with suicidal thoughts and attempts forced me to confront the raw, aching pain I had avoided for so long. Seeking help taught me that laughter can coexist with loss, that healing isn't linear, and that mental health struggles are not something of which to be shameful. Most importantly, I learned the doorway marked "Suicide" wasn't my only path to what I thought would be peace. There were other paths that required work, patience, and faith. And while the storm still rages sometimes, I've learned how to weather it, finding light in places I never expected.

Through confronting my mental health struggles, I found the strength to choose life; more importantly, I chose myself. I chose to break the cycles of silence, shame, and generational pain that defined so much of my past. It wasn't easy, and it wasn't instant, but each step forward was a radical act of self-love and defiance against everything that tried to destroy me.

CHAPTER 20

PURSUIT OF FINANCIAL FREEDOM

ONE CHILLY MORNING ON the way to school, my mother and I were engaged in one of our regular arguments, the kind that left both of us exasperated and shouting over each other. This clash revolved around money, or more accurately, the lack thereof. My fifteen-year-old self was growing frustrated with hand-me-down clothes from my Aunt Miranda. My budding body no longer fit into her petite throwaways, and I felt like a walking billboard for our struggles.

"I'm tired of looking like this!" I snapped, my voice louder than I intended. "Why can't I have nice clothes like everyone else?"

"My job is to provide your needs, not your wants," she replied sharply, her patience thinning.

"Well, if you're providing my needs, why don't I have decent clothes?" I shot back, my words laced with the unfiltered selfishness only a teenager can master.

She sighed; her tone resigned. "You have clothes, Tina. They may not be what you want, but they cover you, don't they?"

Her words lit a fire in me, and as the car pulled up to my high school, I jumped out and slammed the door without another word. Drama queen, maybe, but I had reached my breaking point. I was tired of being teased for looking homeless, tired of wearing ill-fitting clothes, tired of feeling like the world could see how much we struggled. As her car disappeared down the road, I decided I wasn't going to school that day. Instead, I hauled my butt home, my backpack slapping against my back with every determined step. Three miles later, I stumbled into the house, startling my mother as she stood in the kitchen.

"What the hell are you doing, Tina?" she gasped, her eyes wide with confusion.

"I'm getting a job today!" I declared, still breathless from my brisk three-mile walk, for which I hadn't trained. "And I'm not coming home until I have one."

Her expression was a mix of disbelief and amusement, but I didn't wait for her to respond. I showered, pulled my hair back into what I thought was a professional bun, borrowed a skirt and blouse from Mama's closet, and grabbed a notebook and pen. With no bus fare, I set off on foot toward the Rancho Cordova shopping plaza five miles away, convinced that I would find a job before the day was over.

The walk felt endless, each step dragging against the ache in my feet, and the gnawing hunger rumbling within. My determination burned brighter than the discomfort. Store by store, I stepped inside, straightened my borrowed blouse, and politely asked the same question: "Are you hiring?" Most responses were some variation of, "We're always accepting applications," which I quickly realized was a polite way of saying no. I refused to let it discourage me. With each rejection, I squared my shoulders and pushed forward, my resolve unshakable. I was on a mission, and nothing, not the blisters forming on my heels or the low rumble of hunger in my belly, was going to stop me.

By late morning, I had collected a stack of twenty applications and carried them like trophies, a physical reminder of my progress. My legs felt like lead as I trudged toward my friend Javier's apartment, a sanctuary destination I hadn't planned but desperately needed. Javier greeted me with his familiar soft grin, the kind that made me feel welcome, with no need to say a word. To the outside world, Javier was the archetype of a gangster. His face and neck tattoos told stories of a life the world assumed they understood, and his crisp, perfectly pressed Dickies pants, white tank top, and spotless, meticulously laced white Converse only reinforced the image. A neatly folded bandana hung from his back pocket, its edges sharp and deliberate, a subtle but unmistakable signal of his affiliations. To me, all of that was surface-level. I didn't see the stereotype. I saw the kind-hearted, well-mannered friend who always treated me with a level of respect and regard that felt rare and precious. Javier was the person who could carry the weight of the world on his shoulders yet still find the time to make me feel like I mattered.

He waved me inside as if he'd been expecting me, even though I had shown up completely unannounced.

"What's up, Dimples?" he said casually, using the nickname he and his friends had given me.

177

It always made me smile, partly because it was true - my dimples were impossible to miss, and partly because it felt like a badge of acceptance in a world where I didn't quite belong.

Javier stepped aside, letting me into the small apartment that smelled faintly of laundry detergent and something spicy simmering on the stove. His calm presence immediately made me feel at ease, like I'd found a pocket of safety in the madness of my day. For all the assumptions people made about him, Javier never let the outside world define who he was. While he moved around the kitchen, I set to work. I spread the applications across the table like a student preparing for an exam, carefully filling in each blank space with my best handwriting. The silence was comforting, broken only by the sound of Javier cooking. He didn't ask why I was there or why I wasn't at school; he just let me focus. That simple, unspoken understanding meant more to me than I could say.

When he placed a plate of food in front of me, the smell alone made me realize how hungry I was. I ate quickly but with gratitude, the warmth of the meal giving me the energy to power through the rest of the applications. By the time I finished, my hand ached, but my heartfelt lighter. As I gathered my things, Javier disappeared into the kitchen for a moment and returned with a small plastic sandwich bag filled with five dollars in quarters.

"Be safe out there, Dimples," he remarked with a soft smile as he handed it to me.

I stared at the bag for a moment, the weight of his kindness hitting me harder than I expected. It wasn't just the quarters, it was the thoughtfulness, the care he'd shown in such a simple gesture.

"Thank you," I responded, feeling a wave of gratitude.

Javier shrugged it off like it was nothing, but to me, it was everything. With his help, I left his apartment recharged and ready for the next part of my journey. His kindness stayed with me, a reminder that even in the toughest moments, there were people who cared.

I spent the rest of the day returning applications and gathering manager's names and numbers for follow-ups. Some businesses told me they weren't hiring, others said they didn't hire minors, something they could've mentioned the first time around. Still, I kept going. By the time I reached the bus stop, my feet felt like they were on fire. Sitting down was a relief I hadn't realized I needed.

Over the next three weeks, I methodically called every business on my list twice a week. One by one, they crossed themselves off, offering the same flat rejection: "We're not hiring." With each call, my hope dwindled, but I refused to give up. By the end, only one place hadn't said no, The International House of Pancakes, now simply known as IHOP. Every week, I stopped by, called, and checked in with the manager, Frank.

Each time, he gave me the same polite but dismissive answer: "We don't have anything yet."

Whether it was persistence or sheer stubbornness, I would not let up. Finally, after weeks of determined follow-ups, my persistence paid off, or maybe I just wore Frank down. Either way, he finally said the words I'd been waiting to hear: "Come in for an interview next week."

From the moment I hung up the phone, I was consumed with preparing for the interview. Every day leading up to it, I planned and re-planned my outfit in meticulous detail. Should I wear the blouse with the button or borrow an outfit from my friend Tammy? Long or mid length skirt, hair up or down? Each night, I practiced applying the little makeup I knew how to use to perfection in front of the bathroom mirror, ensuring a polished but not overdone look. Mama even got involved in running mock interviews with me after school. She played the role of a no-nonsense manager, throwing curveball questions at me to make sure I stayed calm under pressure. I rehearsed my answers until they came out smooth and confident, though my nerves remained firmly intact.

The day of the interview, I walked into IHOP feeling equally nervous and prepared. Frank greeted me with a firm handshake, and I could see the faint glimmer of approval in his eyes as he sized me up. I sat across from him, keeping my back straight and my smile steady, and answered each of his questions with the poise of someone far older than fifteen. By the end of the interview, Frank leaned back in the booth and nodded.

"As soon as you get your work permit from your school, I will add you to the schedule," he declared.

Just like that, my determination had paid off. I was officially an IHOP hostess. The pride I felt in that moment was overwhelming. I had set a goal, worked for it tirelessly, and earned it all on my own. It wasn't just a job; it was proof that I could rely on myself and make my way in the world.

I felt a sense of true accomplishment for the first time. For six months, I threw myself into the job, learning the ins and outs of customer service, greeting customers with a smile, and earning every paycheck with a pride I hadn't felt before. It wasn't just about the money; it was about proving to myself that I could stand on my own. Then, one day, at the start of my shift, Frank called me into his office. The uncertain look on his face immediately set my nerves on edge. Something was wrong. I could feel it. My mind raced through every mistake I could've made. Had I messed up the register? Forgotten to clock out? The tension in the air was palpable as I sat down across from him.

Frank sighed, his shoulders slumping slightly, and I braced myself for whatever was coming.

"I just got off the phone with corporate," he began, his tone apologetic. "And... they told me I shouldn't have hired you."

The words hit like a gut punch. My pit formed in my stomach as he explained further.

"Apparently, company policy says employees have to be at least sixteen years old." He shook his head in frustration. "And you're only fifteen."

I couldn't believe it. After all the hard work I'd put in, all the effort I'd given to prove myself, a technicality was pulling the rug out from under me.

Frank's voice softened as he continued. "I'm so sorry. This is on me. I should've caught it. You've been a great addition to the team, and this has nothing to do with your performance. I promise, as soon as you turn sixteen, the job is yours again."

His apology was genuine, and I could tell he felt terrible, but it didn't soften the blow. With tears in my eyes, I nodded, fighting to maintain my composure.

"I understand," I replied, even though part of me didn't.

I had finally found something that made me feel capable and independent, and now it was slipping away through no fault of my own.

My wait to return stretched to seven endless weeks, but after my rehiring, I worked harder than ever. I moved from host to server, then to crew chief, and even trained as a cook. That job wasn't just a source of income; it was a symbol of my independence, my determination to prove I could rely on myself.

Turning sixteen didn't just mean getting my job back, it meant a whole new level of freedom. It was the age when I could finally get my driver's permit, and eventually, my license. The thought of no longer being tethered to the bus schedule, of being able to come and go on my own terms, filled me with determination. With Mama's guidance and impeccable patience, I learned how to drive, practicing in parking lots and quiet streets until the feel of the wheel in my hands became second nature. Having a license wasn't enough. I needed a car.

For three months, I saved relentlessly, squirreling away every paycheck, every tip, and every spare dollar I could get my hands on. Each week, Mama took me to the bank, and I handed over my hard-earned cash with a sense of purpose that filled me with excitement. Walking out with that fresh balance slip in my hand was the best part. It was proof that I was getting closer to my dream. Watching my account grow, little by little, left me bursting with pride and anticipation. It wasn't just about the money; it was about what it represented: freedom, independence, and the promise of something for which I had worked so hard.

Finally, after months of saving, I bought my first car. To call it a car might've been generous. It was a relic, a Ford Wagon LTD mini station wagon. It was a beast of a vehicle with a primer-gray exterior that appeared sanded down and forgotten about, with a maroon interior that had seen better days. The driver's window was stuck in a state of defiance. It wouldn't roll up or down without a fight. I had to shove it down with one hand and pull it back up with the other, an awkward dance that became part of the car's personality. The radio and tape player required a firm shove to work, and the engine had a rattle that announced my presence long before my arrival. None of that mattered. To me, it was perfect. That car wasn't just a vehicle; it was a symbol of everything I had worked for, my independence, my determination, my refusal to let circumstances dictate my life. It wasn't just a car; it was freedom on four wheels.

When I sat in the driver's seat, gripping the worn steering wheel, I didn't see the lack of paint or hear the engine's imperfections. I didn't care that the windows rattled when I drove over a bump or that the air conditioning had long since given up. To me, that Ford Wagon was a luxury car, a chariot of freedom.

My car was ugly, old, and loud, but it was also beautiful to me. It represented a turning point in my life that changed my circumstances and would shape my future, one bumpy mile at a time. When I drove it, I wasn't just going from place to place. I was moving forward, carving out a life where I called the shots, and nothing, not even an old, clunky car, could take that away from me.

Reflecting on that time of my life, those months of determination taught me far more than how to earn a paycheck. They taught me about the delicate balance between independence and emotional fulfillment. Saving every dollar and achieving my goal of buying a car was empowering, no doubt. It gave me a sense of control in a world that had so often felt overwhelming and uncertain. Still, it didn't heal the deeper wounds I carried, wounds left by years of mistrust, neglect, and disappointment.

Hurting had become second nature to me, a constant companion. Over time, I had built walls around myself: thick, impenetrable walls designed to keep the pain out. Those same walls kept everything else out, too: connection, love, trust. Earning money and buying my car felt like I was proving to the world, and to myself, that I didn't need anyone. But deep down, I couldn't ignore the emptiness that lingered. No amount of independence could fill the hollow spaces left by a lack of support or guidance. Despite that, it was a start. That car, as flawed and clunky as it was, symbolized more than just freedom. It was a small but significant step toward reclaiming a sense of control in my life. It was proof I could set a goal, work relentlessly for it, and make it happen on my own terms.

The journey was tiresome, yet incomplete. As much as I prided myself on my newfound independence, I couldn't ignore the truth: independence wasn't the same as healing. The walls I built around myself may have protected me from disappointment, but they also kept me isolated in my pain. I was beginning to realize that taking charge of my life wasn't just about earning money or achieving goals; it was about letting those walls down, piece by piece, so I could start letting the good in, too.

That realization wouldn't come all at once. In fact, it would take many years to chip away at those pieces. The seeds, however, had been planted, with my first car, my first steps into independence. The beginning of something bigger; it showed me I had the strength to navigate life's challenges, even if I didn't have all the answers yet. In that, there was hope, a glimmer of light breaking through the cracks in the walls I had worked so hard to build.

"Your greatest strength is your realness, the kind that makes fake people uncomfortable and the authentic inspired."
Her Empowering Mindset
— Case Kenny

PART 5
TURNING POINTS AND TRANSFORMATION

CHAPTER 21

THE STRENGTH WITHIN

IN MY YOUTH, I endured a level of bullying and abuse that exceeded anything a child should have to bear. Neither home nor school offered a sanctuary, leaving me to navigate a world where safety felt unattainable. As a tall, gap-toothed, frizzy-headed mixed girl, with a large nose, I stood out like a neon sign flashing "target." My unruly hair, which my mother had no clue how to manage, seemed to amplify my differences. My insecure, timid demeanor made me an easy mark.

At school, the torment came in fierce waves, name-calling, cruel taunts, exclusion, and the occasional shove or trip in the hallway. Kids would point and laugh, their words sharp and deliberate, cutting me down with insults that echoed long after the school bell rang.

"Nobody loves you!" they'd shout.

"Your parents don't even want you. You should just kill yourself!"

Each word hit like a dagger, slicing through the fragile threads of my self-esteem. I'd bite the inside of my cheek, willing myself not to cry, but their laughter burrowed deep, leaving me feeling small, powerless, and utterly invisible.

Even though Curtis was no longer a part of my life, the shadow of his cruelty loomed over me, his rejection and abuse replaying in my mind with every insult hurled my way. The disdain in the kid's voices felt eerily familiar, as if they were picking up where he had left off. Each cruel comment brought back memories of his cold, dismissive tone, and the pain that never seemed to truly fade.

The mistreatment I endured surrounded me like a suffocating fog, seeping into every corner of my life. There was no space to breathe, no space to feel safe. At school, I was a target. At home, memories of the past haunted me. No matter where I turned, it felt like the world was intent on reminding me I didn't belong, leaving me struggling to find even the smallest sliver of light in the overwhelming darkness.

Even amid all that pain, I learned to adapt. By my freshman year of high school, I decided if I couldn't escape the bullying, I would stop it by becoming the bully myself. It wasn't a conscious decision at first; it was survival. I'll never forget the guilt I felt bullying Ashley for cupcakes in elementary school, and for a long time after that, I avoided picking on anyone, but high school brought its own kind of torture. It was kill or be killed, and the stakes felt higher. I lashed out at others, mimicking the very behavior that had caused me so much harm. I felt a twisted sense of control in those moments, as though flipping the script would shield me from the torment.

Verbal insults had always been the extent of my bullying, but one day, I crossed a line I never thought I'd reach. One chilling incident stands out like a scar in my memory, a moment that still makes my insides crawl when I think about it. In gym class, I was desperate to be part of a clique of girls I considered cool. They had taken me under their wing, and I was eager to prove myself and finally belong.

Their target that day was Raven, a shy freshman who always kept to herself. She was an easy target: large glasses that slipped down her nose, an awkward gait, and hair that looked as though no one had ever taught her how to care for it. The girls started mocking her, laughing about her "nappy hair" and the way she walked, their words cruel and unrelenting.

I joined in, eager for their approval. The words came out of my mouth, sharp and cutting, and for a moment, their laughter felt like validation. As I watched Raven's face crumble under the weight of our insults, a bullet of shame shot through me. Each word I hurled at her landed like a stone, and I couldn't ignore the familiar sting. Many times before, others had thrown those same words at me. And yet, I did not stop. I used their laughter as fuel, pushing aside the gnawing guilt in favor of acceptance.

As if the verbal assault wasn't enough, one girl muttered, "She's trash," and the words lit a dangerous spark in me.

"Let's put her where she belongs," I said, the idea forming before I even realized what I was saying.

As we left the gym, with students milling about and the crowd's attention turning toward us, I made my move. I overpowered Raven, grabbing her small frame and flipping her into one of the giant aluminum trash cans by the door. It happened so fast, I barely registered what I was doing until it was over. Laughter erupted around me, and for a moment, I felt what I thought was triumph.

When I looked at her, I could see horror and humiliation frozen on Raven's face; tears filled her wide eyes, but her pride prevented her from letting them fall. In that instant, something inside me shattered. I had thought this would earn me respect, maybe even admiration, or at least get people to leave me alone. And in a way, it worked. After that day, people stopped messing with me, at least to my face. The victory felt hollow, and the shame hit me like a tidal wave. As I walked away, I couldn't shake the image of her face. The look in her eyes was one I knew all too well. It was the same look I'd had countless times when I was the one being bullied. The laughter I craved now sounded cruel and empty. I realized I had become the very thing I despised.

The burden of my actions haunted me for weeks, weighing heavily on my conscience. In all honesty, I remain ashamed of my decision and the psychological damage she endured because of me. I could not sleep or concentrate. My eyelids would shut, and there she'd be in the trash, a stark reminder of the pain I had caused. The respect I believed I had earned proved costly. The worst part was that I knew exactly how she felt. I had experienced feelings of insignificance, worthlessness, and invisibility. I vowed never to let anyone hurt me like that again, yet I ended up hurting someone else the same way.

That realization became a turning point for me. Living like this was no longer an option. I couldn't keep taking part in a cycle of cruelty just to protect myself. Even if it meant being bullied again, I promised myself I would stop hurting others. I wish I could say it was an overnight transformation - far from it. It was, however, the beginning of a shift in how I saw myself and the world around me. Raven's pain mirrored my own, and it taught me a lesson I'd carry with me for the rest of my life: people that have been hurt often become people who hurt others.

Simply put, echoing the amazing Joyce Meyer's famous words, "Hurting people hurt people."

It would be a long road, but I resolved to be the one to stop the pattern. Looking back, being bullied left a mark on me that ran much deeper than bruised feelings or hurt pride. It embedded itself into my sense of self-worth, shaping how I saw the world and where I believed I fit within it. The name-calling, isolation, constant reminders that I wasn't good enough, it all chipped away at me until I believed them. I carried that pain silently, internalizing every insult and rejection. And when you carry that kind of pain for long enough without a safe place to release it, it festers. It grows heavy, and sometimes, it turns into something else entirely.

For me, that something else was becoming the thing I once feared: a bully. It didn't happen overnight. But slowly, I found that if I was the one making others feel small; I didn't feel as invisible. There was power in being the one people didn't mess with. Power in making others laugh at someone else's expense instead of watching them laugh at me. It gave me a twisted sense of control in a life where I otherwise felt powerless.

That power was short-lived, and it came at a cost. Every time I lashed out at someone else, I felt more ashamed of who I was becoming. I knew what it felt like to be on the receiving end of cruelty. I knew the sting of exclusion and the pain of not being believed or protected. Yet, in my desperation to protect myself, I recreated that same pain in others. It was a cycle I didn't fully understand at the time, but one I eventually came to recognize for what it was: a survival tactic born from trauma.

Both roles, victim and aggressor, had complicated and heavy psychological effects. As a victim, I developed deep empathy, and as an aggressor, I carried guilt. That duality haunted me for a long time. It made it hard to trust myself, to know where I stood on the moral scale. Healing required me to face both parts of that story. To forgive the scared, wounded child who lashed out, and to show compassion to the younger version of myself who just wanted to be seen, accepted, and safe.

Breaking that cycle, choosing kindness, choosing to be a protector instead of a perpetrator, was one of the most important decisions I ever made. It wasn't easy. It meant facing hard truths about myself and the pain I carried. But it also meant reclaiming my power in a new way, one rooted in love, strength, and accountability. And that made all the difference.

Once I became a parent, I made a solemn vow: the pain I had experienced would not be passed down to my children. No matter how difficult, I was determined to break the cycle of trauma and hurt. I wanted my children to feel safety, love, and security in ways I had never known. I promised myself that their lives would be different, brighter, and free from the shadows that had darkened my childhood.

Wanting to do something and knowing how to do it are two entirely different things. I carried so much unhealed trauma, so many unresolved wounds, that no matter how well-intentioned I was, it inevitably spilled over into my parenting. In my desperate efforts to protect my children from the pain I had endured, I swung too far to the other extreme. I became overprotective, guarding them fiercely from any perceived threat, no matter how small or how necessary.

At the time, I thought I was doing the right thing. I thought shielding them from the world's harshness would spare them from the heartache I had known. When I rewind the past, I can see how my actions sometimes did more harm than good. By trying to control every detail of their lives, I unintentionally stifled their growth. I let my fears dictate my parenting, creating boundaries that weren't always about keeping them safe, but about keeping me comfortable. For example, I would go to great lengths to ensure they didn't face rejection or disappointment, intervening in situations where they might have learned resilience or independence. If they struggled with friendships, I tried to fix it. If they failed at something, I softened the blow instead of letting them learn from it. I was so focused on preventing their pain that I forgot the value of letting them navigate life on their own terms.

Then there were the days when my unresolved anger and frustration from my past seeped through, moments of which I'm not proud. Times when my patience ran thin, and I reacted out of fear or stress rather than love and understanding. I strived to be an amazing mother, and in many ways, I was. However, I would be remiss if I didn't acknowledge the times I fell short, the times my own unhealed wounds

190

caused unnecessary grief for my children. There were nights I lay awake replaying the day in my head, agonizing over an episode where I let my temper flare or failed to show up for them emotionally in the way they deserved. I wanted so badly to be the mother they needed, but I didn't always have the tools or the awareness to get it right.

As a single mother of three in my late twenties, I purposefully confronted my past trauma. This proved to be one of the most arduous tasks I have ever undertaken. That decade-long process became an emotional roller coaster ride that not only I had to endure but my children and close family had to experience as well. It forced me to sit with memories that made my chest ache and navigate emotions that threatened to drown me. Through it all, I've learned that healing isn't linear, it's messy, painful, and unpredictable.

Reflecting on those vital years, I realize that breaking the cycle isn't about being a perfect parent, it's about being a willing one. A willing parent acknowledges their flaws, faces their own pain, and commits to doing better. It took time, therapy, and a lot of soul-searching to understand that healing myself was just as important as rearing my children. The work wasn't easy, and it wasn't quick, but it was necessary. Through the mistakes and missteps, I learned that love isn't about shielding them from every hardship; it's about equipping them to face life with strength, empathy, and self-worth. Instead of controlling their environment, I eventually concentrated on guiding them through it. I tried to show them it is okay to make mistakes, that pain is part of growth, and that no matter what, I would always be there to support them.

I'm proud of the mother I became, not because I was perfect, but because I was committed. Committed to learning, to growing, and to ensuring that the cycle of abuse ended with me. Although my past burdens me, I know my children bear a lighter load; they know they are loved, valued, and free to be themselves. That is the legacy I fought to give them.

As I think about my journey, I can see how far I've come. I've turned my pain into purpose, using my experiences to teach my children the importance of kindness, empathy, and breaking cycles. I've committed to helping, not hurting, and to being a protector for those who can't protect themselves. The weight of my past hasn't disappeared, but it no longer defines me. The girl who once threw someone into a trash can out of fear and desperation is gone. In her place stands a woman determined to walk the right path, no matter how difficult it may be, and in that, I've found strength I never knew I had.

CHAPTER 22

EMBRACING INDEPENDENCE

FROM THE TIME I was thirteen years old, I decided I was moving out of my mother's house as soon as possible. The constant uproar at home felt like a storm that never ended: loud, relentless, and unpredictable. Mama's new boyfriend, Shane, was now living with us and his harsh presence only made things worse, as he brought with him a suffocating tension. The arguments between us became a regular soundtrack to my days, each one escalating until the walls vibrated with anger. That unshakable feeling, the overwhelming sense that I was out of place, fueled my resolve. It wasn't just a desire to leave; it was a need. I started researching emancipation laws like it was a full-time job. I was determined to find a way out, but the first thing I learned was that freedom came with a price tag, and I was flat broke.

Not one to give up easily, I started hustling. I'd been making money on and off since I was eight, doing odd jobs like mowing lawns, washing cars, and even selling golf balls. By thirteen, I'd added babysitting to my repertoire, which brought decent money, but not nearly enough to sustain myself. In the meantime, I prepared for my future escape in other ways, by collecting stuff; furniture, household items, and random odds and ends that I imagined would one day fill my first apartment. My mother's three-bedroom duplex, already crowded with a family of five, slowly turned into a storage unit for my dreams. When I finally moved out at seventeen, the house looked half-empty or, as Mama put it, "cleaned out."

My first apartment was at Plaza De Oro in Citrus Heights, California. I moved in with my half-sister Dominique and her toddler, Isaiah. It was the perfect setup. She was a couple years older, and we were still getting to know each other since I hadn't met her until I was ten, when I met my father's side of the family. We thought two strong-willed young women could figure it all out together. Spoiler alert: we were wrong!

Within months, our relationship crumbled under the weight of daily life. I, with all my vast babysitting experience, thought I knew everything about raising a child and was quick to criticize her parenting.

"You shouldn't let Isaiah eat that," I'd say, or, "You need to be stricter with him."

Thinking of how judgmental I was at the time now makes me cringe. Dominique, doing the best she could as a young mother, tolerated my self-righteousness until she couldn't anymore. Our arguments became daily battles, and eventually, she moved out, back home with her mother, Big Dominique.

When she left, I experienced my first real dose of loneliness. I thought independence would feel liberating, but it didn't. The empty apartment echoed my own doubts and insecurities. I craved freedom with every fiber of my being. I dreamed of the day I could escape the bedlam and tension of home, imagining how liberating it would feel to have my own space, my own rules, and my own life. When that day finally came, I realized freedom wasn't as simple or sweet as I envisioned. Then there was the responsibility. For the first time, I was solely responsible for everything: rent, utilities, groceries, and the endless little expenses that seemed to pop up out of nowhere. The burden of it all was heavier than I expected, and I felt it pull every time I opened my wallet. There was no safety net, no backup plan. If I didn't make rent, there wasn't a parent or sibling to step in and save the day. It was all on me.

Around this time, I met Maurice Townsend. He was a new hire at IHOP who transferred in from Texas, and the first time I saw him, I felt a spark. He was tall, slender, and handsome, with a serene confidence that drew people in. Maurice had a way of seeing through my walls, challenging me in ways no one else ever had. Our connection was immediate. We became fast friends, spending hours together both at work and off the clock. He had this way of calling me out on my victim mentality, pointing out when I was making excuses or feeling sorry for myself.

"You're stronger than you act," he told me once during one of our countless arguments in the manager's office. Somehow, even when we clashed, I felt drawn to him.

Maurice became my first love, though "love" might not be the right word. It was more like a twisted fairy tale, the kind that no Disney studio would ever consider. He lived with me for a time, along with his girlfriend, Jenna, and their two kids, Gary and Ronisha. Yes, you read that right. Jenna and the kids lived with us, and I was secretly head over heels for her man. I knew it was wrong, but I was blinded by my feelings for him. I convinced myself that our connection was special, that he would eventually leave her for me.

To say it was messy would be an understatement. It was a full-blown disaster. Maurice and I carried on an affair right under Jenna's nose. We stole moments wherever we could, in my car during late-night drives, in the break room at work, and even in our shared apartment when she wasn't around. It was thrilling and addictive, as well as deeply twisted. I believed that what we had was special, that somehow, we were the exception to the rules of morality and decency.

As if the situation wasn't complicated enough, I became deeply enmeshed in Maurice's family. It wasn't the first time I'd slid seamlessly into someone else's world. I had been doing it since childhood, learning how to adapt and fit wherever I could. Maurice's mother, Felicia, took an immediate liking to me, and before long, she was openly favoring me over Jenna. She would drop brief comments about how I carried myself or how "well-matched" Maurice and I were, and I used her approval to my advantage. Each compliment from her reinforced my conviction that Maurice and I were destined to be together.

My visits to his family's home became more frequent, and soon it felt like I was part of their inner circle. I'd sit on their couch, laugh at their jokes, and share meals with them, all while pretending Jenna didn't exist. Maurice's family started to treat me like I was the girlfriend, and I reveled in the attention. I told myself this was proof I belonged in his life. But no matter how much Felicia and the rest of his family adored me, there was still one glaring obstacle: Jenna.

It all came to a head during one of my unannounced visits to Maurice's parents' house. Maurice's father, James, was sitting in the living room nursing a glass of whiskey when he cut through the tension with a direct question.

"What is it you want?" he inquired, his voice steady and sharp.

I blinked, faking confusion, even though I knew exactly what he meant.

"What do you mean?" I asked, stalling for time.

He leaned forward, locking eyes with me. "What do you think is going to happen with you and Maurice?"

There it was, the question I had been dodging, even from myself. My heart pounded as I sat up straighter, deciding to stop pretending.

"I love him," I said with as much confidence as I could muster. "We want to be together, but he feels trapped. He wants to break up with Jenna, but she has nowhere to go, and he can't just put her out on the street."

As the words hung in the air, I noticed Felicia standing frozen in the kitchen, holding a dishcloth as if she was in the middle of a soap opera. Maurice, who had just walked through the front door, stood still with a look of both relief and shock, clearly unprepared for me to speak so boldly. The room felt like it was crackling with tension, every second stretching into an eternity. James leaned back in his chair, picked up his whiskey, and took a slow sip.

Then, with a nod, he broke the silence. "That's a bad bitch right there! Don't let that one get away!"

For a second, I was so stunned by his choice of words that I couldn't process what he was saying. A bitch? Was that supposed to be a compliment? But as I caught his knowing smirk and the faint approval in his tone, I realized. This was his way of endorsing me!

Maurice broke the awkwardness by asking me to step outside. Frustration quickly replaced the relief I'd seen on his face moments earlier.

"Why did you say all that in front of them?" he hissed, his voice low but heated.

"Because it's the truth, Maurice!" I shot back, my voice trembling with a mix of anger and desperation. "You've been playing games with me, telling me you're going to leave her, but nothing changes. How long am I supposed to wait?"

His hands flew up in frustration. "You think it's that simple? She's the mother of my kids! Where is she supposed to go? I can't just throw her out!"

I crossed my arms, trying to steady my emotions. "Then why keep telling me you want to be with me? Why let me get so involved in your life, your family's life, if you're not willing to actually leave her?"

We went back and forth, our voices rising until they carried into the night air. It was one of those arguments that didn't have a resolution, just two people trying to justify their own feelings in an impossible situation. Deep down, I think we both knew it couldn't work, but neither of us was ready to let go.

"You and the kids can stay, but she has to go." I demanded.

"Where the hell are we supposed to go?"

"Like I said, you and the kids can stay, but Jenna needs to move out of my apartment tonight."

It's clear now just how delusional I was. I thought my love for Maurice could override the dysfunction, that if I loved him enough, everything else would fall into place. But love doesn't work like that. No amount of passion or determination could change the reality of our situation, and trying to force it only caused more pain, for me, for him, and for everyone caught in the middle. James's backhanded compliment that night stuck with me, not because it was flattering, but because it reflected how misguided I had become. I had turned myself into someone I barely recognized, chasing after a relationship that was never meant to be. That night Maurice, Jenna, and their children moved into a motel until they found an apartment. It was both a relief and heartbreak. The wreckage of my choices and the harsh reality that independence and love aren't about clinging to someone else, but about finding inner strength, confronted me.

That night marked the abrupt end of our affair, a final punctuation to a chapter that was as thrilling as it was destructive. We didn't officially "break things off." There were no dramatic goodbyes or tearful promises to move on, but we both knew it was over. The weight of everything that had happened hung in the air between us, unspoken yet undeniable.

The hardest part wasn't the ending itself; it was having to see each other every day at work. IHOP wasn't exactly a sprawling corporate office where you could avoid someone by sitting on opposite sides of the building. It was a tight-knit, bustling restaurant where shifts were chaotic, and every employee crossed paths multiple times a day. The awkwardness was palpable. At first, we avoided each other entirely, slipping by with forced smiles or quick, mumbled acknowledgments. Conversations were strictly professional. If I needed him to fix a customer's order or if there was an issue with the register, I kept my tone clipped and emotionless. It was painful to act like we hadn't shared something so personal, but pretending was the only way to survive.

The silence between us lasted a few weeks, but eventually, cracks formed in the wall we'd put up. It started with small, almost accidental interactions, a quick joke exchanged at the coffee station, a shared laugh over a customer's outrageous order. Those insignificant moments thawed the ice just enough for us to rebuild something that resembled a friendship. It wasn't easy. Awkward pauses and unspoken tension filled our attempts to rebrand our relationship. Every conversation felt like navigating a minefield, careful not to step on the memories we both knew were still there. There were moments when the awkwardness was almost too much to bear, like when a coworker would mention something innocuous about our past, not knowing the tangled history beneath it. We'd both laugh nervously, pretending it didn't sting.

As the months passed, we found a rhythm. Slowly, the awkwardness faded, replaced by a cautious camaraderie. We both understood, without saying, that what had happened between us was in the past, and there was no going back. For the first time, we built a friendship that wasn't based on secrets or stolen moments, but on mutual respect. By the time we settled into a new dynamic, I could feel the weight lifting. The emotions that had once felt so raw were scabbing over, and though I knew the scars would remain, they didn't hurt as much. Maurice and I would never be the same, yet we had found a way to exist in each other's lives without the damaging effects of an affair. In that, there was a strange sense of peace.

Moving out on my own had felt like a ticket to freedom, but I quickly learned that independence wasn't as glamorous as I'd imagined. Living with Dominique taught me I had a lot to learn about relationships and compassion. I thought I was helping by pointing out her flaws. In reality, I was pushing her away. It took years for us to reconcile, but now, our bond is stronger than ever. I can't help but mourn the closeness we missed back then because of my judgment and immaturity.

Then there was Maurice. Loving him was like chasing a mirage, beautiful and enticing but ultimately unattainable. I poured so much of myself into that relationship, hoping it would fill the void inside me. Instead, it only left me feeling emptier. Even through the dysfunction, Maurice taught me valuable lessons. He forced me to look at myself honestly, to see the ways I was holding myself back from moving forward in my life. We lost touch for quite a few years, but social media helped us reconnect. Since then, we've stayed in contact, watching each other's families grow from afar.

Those early experiences of independence were both exhilarating and painful. They showed me that freedom isn't just about leaving home or paying your rent, but rather about taking responsibility for your choices and learning how to grow through your mistakes. My first apartment wasn't just a physical space; it was the beginning of my journey to understanding myself, flaws and all. Even in the disorder, I can see now how those experiences shaped me, by teaching adaptability, accountability, and the importance of building relationships on a foundation of honesty and respect. Independence wasn't just something I earned, it was something I had to learn to live with, one mistake at a time.

CHAPTER 23

MOMENT OF DARKNESS

CONFLICT WAS SOMETHING I had spent my entire life avoiding, even when it meant I would suffer. Throughout my young life, I learned that speaking up didn't bring justice; it made things worse. My life experience thus far had not equipped me with the skills to handle confrontation in a way that protected me. Instead, I became an expert at fleeing, at slipping away from situations rather than addressing them head-on.

That instinct to escape played out once again when I began experiencing sexual harassment at work. My new shift manager at IHOP, Jerome, made every day unbearable, cornering me with crude comments, lingering too close, finding any excuse to touch my shoulders or lower back. Each time I felt his presence behind me, my body became tense. I knew what was coming, a disgusting joke, an inappropriate whisper, a leer that made my skin crawl. Maybe he had heard about Maurice and me and thought he would get in on the action, or maybe he was just a straight creep. Because Maurice now worked days and I worked nights, I had to endure Jerome's toxic behavior with no buffer.

Quitting wasn't an option. I had rent to pay, bills piling up, and no safety net to catch me. Life had already taught me that standing up for myself often led to retaliation, not resolution. So, reporting him to management was not an option in my mind. My usual response kicked in: I ran.

When the company announced they were opening a new IHOP forty minutes away, I volunteered to transfer. The location was inconvenient, and I knew my crappy Ford Wagon LTD had no business making that daily commute, but the alternative - staying and putting up with Jerome, was worse. I was willing to sacrifice time, money, and even the reliability of my barely functioning car just to get away from him.

A couple of months into working at the new location, my car finally called it quits. I was running late for my shift, trying to coax the engine to keep going when, in the middle of a busy intersection, the worst happened. Smoke started billowing from under the hood. My heart sank. The car jerked, sputtered, and died right there, leaving me stranded in the center of a four-way intersection. Horns blared, impatient drivers yelled out of their windows, shaking their heads and throwing up their hands like I had broken down on purpose.

I scrambled out of the car in my full IHOP uniform, an apron-covered dress, nylons clinging to my legs, and orthopedic senior citizen shoes that, despite looking like they belonged to someone's eighty-year-old grandmother, were the most comfortable shoes I had ever worn. Shout out to Claudia, the seasoned career server who had taken one look at my Payless knockoff heels and intervened before I destroyed my feet forever. With no choice but to push my dead car out of traffic, I planted my feet and started shoving with all my might. My arms burned, my legs strained, and I could feel the heat of a thousand impatient stares on my back. Just as I was about to collapse from sheer humiliation and exhaustion, a grown man appeared beside me.

"Need some help?" he asked, already putting his hands on the car.

I nodded breathlessly, too relieved to question his intentions. Together, we got the car out of the way, pushing it onto the shoulder of the road. I exhaled a shaky sigh of relief. Finally, something had gone right.

For a moment, I believed this man had helped me out of pure human decency. That belief lasted approximately three seconds. As I turned to thank him, he held out his hand, palm up, expectantly. His expression had shifted from helpful to impatient, his body language tense. A sinking feeling settled in my stomach. Of course, nothing was free in this world. I fumbled into my apron pocket and pulled out the last ten-dollar bill I had. It was supposed to be my gas money, either to get home or, now that my car was dead, to pay someone else for a ride. Instead, I pressed it into his sweaty, dirty palm, avoiding eye contact.

"Thank you," I mumbled.

His fingers curled around the bill, and for a moment, I thought our interaction was complete.

Then he scoffed. "Is that it?"

I froze, my breath catching in my throat.

"That's all I have, sir," I said quickly, backing toward my car. "Thank you for your help."

Before he could say anything else, I turned and made a beeline for my car to find a quarter and headed to the payphone at the gas station across the street to call someone, anyone, to help me. As I waited at the crosswalk, blinking back frustrated tears, I looked up and saw the man who had just shaken me down standing on the median. He was holding a cardboard sign. I stared, processing what I was seeing. He was homeless.

A part of me wanted to be angry, but the anger faded as quickly as it came. Yes, he had taken my last ten dollars, and yes, I did not know how I was going to get to work, get home, or repeat the process tomorrow. But then I thought about him. That money might mean the difference between a meal that night or going to bed hungry. Regarding the bed, my last ten dollars could have been what he needed for a motel and a warm bed that night. Despite everything, I still had an apartment with a warm futon to collapse onto after what was surely about to be a hell of a day. I'd have food that night, even if it was just my leftover IHOP meal I always saved. It wasn't much, but at that moment, it was enough.

By some miracle, Maurice and his mother came to my rescue. She dropped me off at work and he somehow got my car running long enough to drive it to my apartment, even as it spewed white smoke like a dying dragon. Then, he came back and picked me up after my shift.

The ultimate irony of it all? The person who fixed my car, who got me back on the road so I wouldn't have to keep begging for rides, was Shane, my mother's boyfriend. Shane, whom I had rejected at every turn. Shane, whom I had disrespected and treated like garbage whenever I got the chance. Shane, who, despite all of that, still showed up to help me.

Although Maurice and I were no longer entangled in an intimate relationship, there was an undeniable connection between us, a quiet, unspoken bond that left us vulnerable to each other's needs and happiness. No matter what had transpired between us, we still understood each other in a way that few others did. I had never been good at masking my emotions, and Maurice knew me well enough to see that my stress went far beyond a broken-down car. On the ride home that night, he observed me, his brows furrowing as I fidgeted, avoiding his gaze.

"What's going on with you?" he finally pressed, his voice steady but firm. "It's more than just your car, isn't it?"

I hesitated, swallowing the lump in my throat. Admitting failure had never come easily to me, but the weight of carrying everything alone was suffocating.

"I'm struggling to make rent by myself," I blurted out, exhaling as if I had been holding my breath for days. "I need a roommate."

Saying it out loud felt like a strange relief, even though it also came with an uncomfortable truth. I was the reason Maurice had left in the first place, and here I was, confessing my desperation to the person I had pushed away. Yet with the twisted circumstance of our relationship, he and his family leaving was the best option. Maurice didn't flinch. He simply leaned back, nodding thoughtfully before offering the one line that always seemed to put me at ease.

"Let me see what I can do."

It was classic Maurice, never over-promising, never dismissing, but always making me feel like I wasn't alone. In that instance, that was enough.

The next morning, the ringing of my phone awakened me. Half-asleep, I fumbled to answer.

"Hello?" I mumbled.

Maurice didn't waste time with pleasantries. "My sister Shannon has a friend from college who's looking for a place to live," he blurted. "I've only met her once, but if you want, I can talk to Shannon and see what's up?"

Still groggy, I sat up, already feeling a spark of hope. "Yes, please call her," I responded quickly, the desperation in my voice clarifying that I didn't have the luxury of being picky.

A couple of days later, I heard a firm knock at my front door. When I opened it, I was met by a young woman standing in the hallway, her arms loaded down with a few oversized black trash bags, the entirety of her belongings.

"Are you Christina?" she asked, barely waiting for my nod before thrusting a wad of cash into my hand. "This is for the first month."

"You must be Jayla," I replied, taking the money without hesitation and shoving it into my pocket without even counting it.

At that juncture, a wave of relief washed over me. I could pay my rent, and that was all that mattered. My anxieties over my finances dulled my instincts, causing me to ignore every red flag, like observing all her belongings could fit in the trunk of my car, or the urgency in her voice, the way she paid without asking a single question. None of it mattered. All I knew was that I could breathe for another month. Somehow, that was enough.

Jayla and I operated on opposite schedules, which meant we rarely saw each other, but when we did, the tension was thick enough to cut with a knife. From the start, it was clear we were not a good match. I kept a meticulously clean house. Some might even argue I had a touch of Obsessive Compulsive Disorder (OCD), but Jayla, on the other hand, clearly had no home training. Dishes piled up in the sink, clothes were thrown across the bathroom floor, and cabinet doors were left open as if she had a personal vendetta against closing them. Every time I walked through the apartment, I discovered another mess, another reminder that I had let my financial struggles override my better judgment.

It didn't take long for me to realize that this arrangement wasn't sustainable. The constant clash between my need for order and her complete disregard for it made even the simplest interactions feel exhausting. My rent was due every month, and like it or not, for now, Jayla was helping me keep a roof over my head. So I swallowed my frustration and ignored the gnawing feeling in my gut. Because as much as I hated living like this, I hated the idea of losing my apartment even more.

The rare times we were both home, I stayed in my room, avoiding the anarchy unfolding just beyond my door. Meanwhile, Jayla turned the living room into a full-fledged party zone. Almost every weekend, a rotating cast of guys filled the apartment, smoking weed, drinking, and treating the space like their personal lounge. If I politely asked her to keep the noise down, they would get louder. If I insisted no one smoke inside, she would deliberately hotbox the living room, letting the thick haze seep under my door as if to taunt me. It was a blatant display of disregard, a passive-aggressive challenge for which I was quickly losing patience.

For four weeks, I endured it, gritting my teeth, holding my tongue, and trying to convince myself that putting up with her was a lesser evil compared to struggling alone. With each passing day, my resentment grew. The stench of smoke clung to everything I owned, the constant noise made it impossible to rest, and the overwhelming sense of being disrespected in my home became unbearable. Something had to give, and I knew, eventually, it would.

During the fourth weekend, Maurice and Shannon stopped by for a visit, offering me a brief escape from the tension that had become my daily existence. As soon as they stepped inside, it was clear to see that Jayla and her crew were already deep into their usual routine, the smoke of weed curling in the air, drink glasses scattered across the table, and the thumping of the bass from their music rattling the cheap apartment walls. The entire space reeked of stale beer, bad decisions, and blatant disrespect. Maurice exchanged a look with me, his brows lifting in silent question. *You're dealing with this?* He wrinkled his nose, glancing around in disgust. Rubbing my temples, I sighed before deciding enough was enough.

I walked over to Jayla, who was lounging on the couch like a queen on her throne, half-listening to some guy mumbling through a high-induced haze.

I kept my voice even, controlled. "Jayla, can I talk to you for a second? In private?"

She barely looked up, taking a slow drag of her cigarette before exhaling the smoke in my direction.

"Nah," she said flatly.

I clenched my jaw but kept my tone steady. "Jayla, I need to talk to you now."

That's when she snapped. She jumped up, her voice slicing through the air like a blade.

"Whatever you want to say to me, say it right here! If you got a problem, take your ass to your room and leave us alone!"

I took a slow breath, forcing calm into my voice. "I'm asking you one more time. Come talk to me. Now!"

She glared at me, chest heaving, then turned to her friends and laughed like this was some kind of joke. Her defiance ignited something in me, but I swallowed it down.

"Fine, then y'all need to leave," I firmly stated to her guests.

That got her attention. Jayla lost it. "You don't get to tell my friends shit!" she screamed, stepping toward me like she was ready to throw down. "This is my place too!"

I tilted my head, raising a brow. "No, Jayla. It's my name on the lease, and if you can't respect that, you need to start packing."

Her face turned an alarming shade of red, her fists balling at her sides. She wasn't used to me standing up to her, and I could see the rage simmering beneath the surface. Trying to keep things from escalating further, I took a step back.

"Listen, this isn't working. You have two weeks to figure out where you're going, but your friends, they're done. No more smoking, no more drinking, no more disrespecting my home."

Jayla was practically vibrating with fury now, her nostrils flaring. She turned on her heel and stomped toward her room, muttering a string of expletives under her breath.

I followed, stopping just inside her doorframe. "Look, I'm sorry, but I've had enough."

She whipped around, eyes burning with hatred. "You're a bitch!" she shrieked, and before I could even react, she slammed the door into my body, hard.

The impact forced me back a step, a sharp sting radiating from my shoulder where the door had clipped me. That's when something inside me snapped. The calm, composed version of myself disappeared in an instant. The years of swallowing my anger, of avoiding conflict, of letting people walk all over me, all of it, boiled over in a flash. I didn't think. I felt, and what I felt in that moment was rage.

It all detonated in a single, uncontrollable burst. I don't remember deciding to kick in the door. It just happened. One second, I was standing there, reeling from the impact of it slamming in my face, and the next, my foot connected with the wood like I was leading a SWAT raid. The flimsy doorframe gave way instantly, the sound of splintering wood cracking through the air like a gunshot. Then all hell broke loose.

I charged Jayla with no regard for logic, consequences, or safety. There was no hesitation, no second thoughts, just raw, unfiltered rage exploding from deep inside me. She barely had time to react before I was on her, fists flying. We fought, or at least, she tried to fight. She got a few hits in, but they barely registered. The surge of adrenaline coursing through me made me untouchable, unstoppable. Every ounce of frustration, every moment of disrespected boundaries, every instance of being walked over and dismissed, it all came out at once.

Her face became my only target, and I hit the bullseye every time. I don't know how many times I swung, maybe five, maybe ten, maybe twenty, but I knew one thing for certain: she had started this fight with a nose ring and ended it without one. What felt like a brutal, drawn-out, nine-round battle was actually over in mere seconds. A rush of movement. Yelling. Arms grabbing at me. Suddenly, I was off Jayla, being pulled away by sheer force. Maurice and three of Jayla's male friends struggled to break us apart, their combined weight finally pulling me back as my fists still twitched, ready to strike.

"Christina!" Maurice's voice sliced through the haze, the panic in his tone forcing me back to the present.

I stood there, panting, sweat sticking to my skin, my vision tunneling as reality set in. Two men had each of my arms pinned, another stood behind me with his arms wrapped around my waist like I was a wild animal they were trying to contain. Maurice stood directly in front of me, his hands gripping my face, forcing me to look at him. My chest quivered, my knuckles ached, and my body buzzed like an exposed electrical wire.

"Get the fuck off me!" I yelled, shaking them off.

One by one, they released me, cautiously stepping back like they weren't entirely sure I was done. I turned, surveying the wreckage I had left behind. The door dangled from the bottom hinge, barely hanging on. The room was a disaster. Sheets crumpled, furniture knocked askew. Amidst it all was Jayla. With legs outstretched, she leaned against the wall, blood staining her face. Shannon knelt beside her, pressing a t-shirt against her nose, whispering something I couldn't hear. Jayla's eyes met mine, wide with something I had never seen from her before: fear. The sight of it hit me like a cold slap. I had seen that look before. I had worn that look before, and for the first time in my life, I wasn't on the receiving end of it.

I stepped over the broken door, my legs suddenly feeling weak beneath me, and made my way to my bedroom. Sinking into the corner of my futon, my mind raced. In the background, I could hear Maurice barking orders, his voice urgent, but the words muffled beneath the roar in my head. My pulse was deafening in my ears. The cops are coming, was my first thought. They must be. I pictured the flashing red and blue lights, the heavy weight of handcuffs clicking around my wrists, the cold metal bench in the back of a squad car. Assault, battery, attempted murder. I could already hear the charges in my head. My lack of control was unprecedented, and the fallout was on its way.

A few minutes later, Maurice appeared in my doorway. I braced myself, fully expecting a police officer to be behind him. But he was alone.

I swallowed hard. "Where are they?"

Maurice furrowed his brow. "Where are who?"

I blinked, my throat a desert. "The cops."

A slow smirk spread across his face. "Ain't no cops, Christina. She's not pressing charges; she's so high and drunk she'd be going to jail too."

I exhaled, the tension in my shoulders releasing just a fraction. I wasn't sure if it was relief or confusion that hit me first. Maurice sat beside me, his expression a mix of concern and excitement.

"You okay?" he asked, his voice unusually animated.

I looked at him, still dazed. "What the hell just happened?"

Maurice let out a short laugh, shaking his head. "You just whupped Jayla's ass! You don't remember?"

I frowned. "The last thing I remember is her slamming the door in my face."

Maurice's eyes widened. "You blacked out?"

His voice had the same energy as a sports commentator reliving a championship match. He leaned forward, throwing his hands up in exaggerated motion as he began replaying the entire fight, blow by blow, with all the enthusiasm of someone recounting a legendary fight scene from Rocky. His words blurred together as my mind tried to catch up. I had completely blacked out, and that realization terrified me.

That night, Jayla packed up and left. No cops, no charges, no more fights. It was over. Legally, I walked away unscathed. Psychologically? Not so much. That night stayed with me. Not just because of the violence, but because I lost myself. I had let my anger take over, and in doing so, I had crossed a line I never thought I would. I vowed to never allow myself to lose control like that again.

It was safe to say I had terrible luck with roommates. First, my sister, then Maurice and his entire family, and now Jayla. Each event was a unique disaster, a distinct type of mayhem, as if the universe were conducting a social experiment to determine my breaking point. I had convinced myself that once Jayla was gone, my drama with roommates was finally behind me. I had earned my peace, right? No more sharing my space with messy, disrespectful, or downright infuriating people. I was free.

Eventually, I joined the Army. As it turns out, the universe wasn't done messing with me yet. In fact, it had just been warming up. If I thought dealing with difficult roommates in my apartment was bad, I did not know what was waiting for me in the barracks. Sharing a room with multiple strangers in a high-stress environment and forced cohabitation with people I didn't get to choose. Turns out, the universe has a hell of a sense of humor, and it was about to get the last laugh.

CHAPTER 24

BREAKING POINT

BY MY SENIOR YEAR of high school, my life was a carefully orchestrated whirlwind of disorder. I was up by 6:00 AM every morning, juggling school, volunteer work, and my job at IHOP, where I closed the restaurant almost every night. By the time I got home, it was past midnight, leaving me just a few hours to wind down, possibly knock out my homework that was piling up like dirty laundry, and sleep before the cycle repeated itself.

At first, it wasn't so bad. I was young, fueled by ambition and sheer stubbornness. I had enrolled in an occupational program that allowed me to split my time between school and real-world experience. The first half of the year, I took early childhood development courses and volunteered in elementary schools, working with children, a job that came naturally to me. In the second half, I shifted gears and took an introduction to the medical field class, volunteering in the pediatric ward at the local hospital. That was harder. Seeing kids sick and in pain gutted me, but I found purpose in making them smile, even if just for a moment.

But as the year dragged on, the delicate balancing act I had pieced together unraveled. School, once a priority, had slipped into the background, and survival had taken its place. At seventeen, I was completely on my own - no savings, no help, and no backup plan. Thanks to my terrible luck with roommates, I had burned through every option and was now left with none. No stability, no clear direction, and no idea what in the world I was supposed to do after graduation. The future loomed ahead, an empty, uncertain void, and for the first time, I was terrified.

At a routine meeting with my school counselor to discuss my post-graduation plans, she gave me the final gut punch.

"Christine," she said.

"It's Christina," I replied with irritation, correcting her once again.

In each meeting, she seemed to forget that my name ended with an A, not an E.

"Christina," she replied and began again with a tight-lipped smile, "There's really no need for you to take the SATs or ACTs. You are not college material."

She wasn't being cruel, just matter-of-fact, as if she were reminding me to bring an umbrella on a rainy day. In all honesty, I didn't even flinch. I had believed for years that I wasn't smart enough for college. Throughout most of my schooling, I had trouble keeping up and was eventually put into special education classes. In my mind, the counselor's words weren't an insult, they were confirmation of what I already knew about myself. The real problem was, what now? Most of my friends were either working dead-end jobs or having babies and were on welfare. Neither of those paths appealed to me. The prospect of being trapped in the same cycle of hardship I'd witnessed growing up terrified me, and I knew fast food wasn't the permanent career path I wanted. I wanted more, but what more looked like? I did not know.

Being placed in special education gave me a complex that haunted me for years. It was confirmation that I wasn't smart. It chipped away at my self-esteem and made me second-guess myself at every turn. Every time I misspelled a word or couldn't follow a conversation about something that seemed like common knowledge, I felt inadequate, like I was behind, ignorant, and incapable of catching up.

But life has a way of backing you into a corner, and sometimes, that's exactly what it takes to make you come out swinging. As a single mother struggling to survive with three young sons, I reached a turning point. I realized that if I wanted to do more than just scrape by, if I wanted to thrive, for myself and for my boys, I had to take a leap. So I did.

I enrolled in Thomas Nelson Community College in Virginia, originally pursuing business management, but eventually shifting to early childhood development. My plan was simple: build the foundation I'd need to open a successful daycare after my military service. What I didn't expect was how much I'd enjoy learning, or how good I'd be at it.

The girl who once believed she was dumb, who shrank in classrooms and silenced herself in conversations, graduated with honors. It turns out I wasn't slow or stupid. I was underestimated, even by myself.

My experience with the military also tested me. My brother Lewis, who had joined the Navy, was home on recruiter duty for a few weeks, and when I stopped by to see him, I found him mid-feast, inhaling a six-pack of tacos from his favorite restaurant Del Taco like he was in a competitive eating contest.

Between bites, he looked up at me, completely serious. "You should check it out."

I raised an eyebrow. "Check what out?"

He gestured vaguely with a half-eaten taco. "The Navy."

I scoffed, wrinkling my nose. "The Navy?"

He shrugged, shoving the rest of the taco into his mouth like he hadn't eaten in days.

"Why not? You need some discipline, and this could be a way out."

I gasped, clutching my chest in mock offense. "Excuse me? I need discipline?"

He gave me a deadpan look, wiping hot sauce off his fingers. "You literally just told me you're failing high-school, broke, and about to be couch surfing. Tell me again how 'structured guidance' isn't something you need."

As much as I wanted to argue, even I couldn't deny he had a point. Rude? Absolutely. Accurate? Also, yes.

He invited me to his recruiting station to take a pre-test and see what options might be available. I figured, why not? I had nothing to lose, except, apparently, my dignity, because the way Lewis was looking at me, he knew he won that round.

The next day, I walked into the Navy recruiting office. Lewis and I greeted each other the way we always did, with insults and playful shoves. We had always been physical siblings, rough housing every time we saw each other. I punched him in the arm; he shoved me back harder.

That's when his Station Commander stepped in. "Airmen Knight!" his superior barked. "Get in my office! Now!"

Lewis barely had time to process what was happening before disappearing into the back. Through the thin walls, I could hear muffled yelling, the Station Commander ripping into him for hitting a female civilian, completely unaware that I was his sister.

When Lewis finally reappeared, he looked exasperated. "You just got me chewed out."

I smirked. "That's what little sisters are for."

Pretending to be interested, I listened as the recruiter droned on about the benefits of a Navy career: travel, job security, and education, blah, blah, blah. I nodded along, trying to look serious, but my mind was already drifting. Then he said something that yanked me right back into reality.

"And, of course, you'd have to cut your hair."

I froze mid-nod. "I'm sorry. Did you just say I would have to cut my hair?" I leaned forward, blinking as if I had misheard.

The recruiter, completely unfazed, casually replied, "Well, yeah. Everyone does."

"Yeah, that's not happening!" I snapped, folding my arms.

The poor man looked confused.

"It's just hair. It'll grow back."

I laughed, but not the cheerful kind. It was more of a "you don't know what you're talking about" kind of laugh.

"Listen, Sir. When I was a kid, my mom cut my hair, and I ended up looking like a little boy named Carl. I've been traumatized by that ever since. So, no, I will not be chopping my hair off just to join the Navy."

The recruiter sighed, clearly realizing he had lost this battle. "It's standard policy."

I grabbed my bag and stood. "Well, it was nice meeting you. Good luck with that recruiting thing." And just like that, I walked out, knowing the Navy was not my path.

Lewis barely waited until we got outside before shaking his head.

"So let me get this straight. You're okay with waking up at four AM, getting screamed at, and potentially going to war, but a haircut is where you draw the line?"

I turned to him, completely serious. "One hundred percent."

The very next week, fate stepped in and threw me a curveball. I was sitting in class, only half-paying attention, when an Army recruiter named Staff Sergeant Martinez strode in like he owned the place. He was charismatic, confident, and straight to the point, not to mention easy on the eyes. The type of man who could probably convince someone to sign up for boot camp just by flashing a grin. The way he carried himself, the way he spoke, no fluff, no sugarcoating, just straight facts differed from the over-polished sales-pitch vibe I had gotten from the Navy recruiter.

I sat back, watching as he launched into his presentation, breaking down the ins and outs of Army life. He had slides, statistics, and a tone that implied, I know this isn't for everyone, but if you can handle it, you'll be proud you did it. He talked about discipline. Training. Education benefits. The camaraderie. How the Army transforms you into the person you were meant to be. It was interesting until he started mentioning things like "sacrifices" and "personal adjustments."

That's when I sat up a little straighter, narrowed my eyes, and without a second thought, rudely interrupted the entire presentation.

"Yeah, I hear you, but I have one question," I blurted out, loud enough for the entire class to turn their heads toward me.

Staff Sergeant Martinez, mid-sentence, looked up, a bit taken aback but also amused. "Alright, go ahead."

I cleared my throat and leaned forward, deadly serious. "Do I have to cut my hair?"

The entire room went silent. A few students snickered. Someone muttered, "This girl!"

Staff Sergeant Martinez blinked, then let out a deep, hearty laugh, shaking his head. "Nope."

That was all I needed to hear. I leaned back in my chair, nodded, and crossed my arms.

"Alright, I'm listening," I said, and just like that, my future took a completely unexpected turn.

I agreed to go through the Military Entrance Processing Station (MEPS) and take the ASVAB test, the standardized test that determines which jobs one qualifies for. There was just one problem: I sucked at tests. I struggled to focus for three-hours, my mind constantly drifting. When my results came back, they were bad, so bad that I barely qualified. My recruiter gave me two options: one, retake the ASVAB in sixty days and try for a better score; or two, join with no designated career path, letting the Army assign me a job based on their needs after basic training. By this point, I was within six weeks of losing my apartment and would be homeless before I could retake the test. Barely keeping my life together, I wasn't about to wait around for a retest. I needed out. I chose option two.

There was one more hurdle standing between me and basic training: my weight. I wasn't just a few pounds over; I was so far off the charts that I didn't even qualify for a waiver. That meant no shortcuts, no exceptions. If I wanted to enlist right after graduation, I had two months to lose forty pounds or kiss my Army plans goodbye. The number felt impossible, but if there was one thing I had proven in my life, it was that when I set my mind to something, I made it happen, and I was not about to let this slip away.

From the moment I left that recruiting office, I fully immersed myself in my new mission. I radically changed my diet. Goodbye delicious IHOP pancakes; hello, grilled chicken and tuna. My meals were lean, green, and flavorless, chicken breasts, vegetables, and so much tuna I probably started smelling like the inside of a can. I didn't care, though. I also joined the gym where my other half-brother on my father's side, Alexander, had a membership. He didn't go easy on me;

he trained me like I was already in the Army, pushing me to work harder than I ever had in my life.

"Come on, Christina! You want to be in the Army, or you want to keep making excuses?" he'd shout as I struggled to do a push-up that looked more like a dramatic body flop.

I wasn't just hitting the gym; I was living in it. If I wasn't working or at school, I was working out. Running? Every day. Cycling? Until my legs burned. Push-ups? If you could call them that. If someone had filmed me, I swear it would've gone viral as a Saturday Night Live (SNL) skit. Sit-ups? More like wiggling on the floor until I cried, but I didn't stop. I couldn't. I was obsessed, not just with losing weight, but with proving to myself, and everyone else, that I could do this.

Two months later, I walked back into the recruiting office, my belly clenched with anxiety. I had worked my butt off, but had it been enough? Staff Sergeant Martinez looked me up and down before I even stepped on the scale.

"Alright, let's see," he muttered, motioning for me to step up.

The numbers flickered. The room was silent. Then, his eyebrows shot up, and he let out a low whistle.

"Damn!" He shook his head, barely believing what he was seeing. "You really wanted this."

He did not know. That weigh-in wasn't just about numbers, it was about proving to myself that when I wanted something, nothing and no one could stop me. In that moment, I knew in order to survive; I had to leave to live, and joining the Army was my only way out.

CHAPTER 25

NEW BEGINNINGS

JULY 27TH, 1999, A warm summer evening with a beautiful red and orange sunset that represented more than a routine closure for the current day, was my last day in California before joining the Military. As my family gathered at the bottom of my mother's sloped driveway to say their goodbyes, a mix of pride and trepidation flashed in their eyes. This was more than just leaving home. This was the start of a new life, a chance for me to step out of the shadows of the past and hopefully stumble upon a trail that would lead to a life worth living. And yet, as I hugged my mom tightly, the familiar warmth of her embrace made it hard to let go. Then Grandma Marilyn's arms enveloped me as she had done so many times before, but this time felt different. For a moment, the discouraging words my family repeated in my mind on loop paused. Their fearful statements of doubt about me making it in the Army and how I would not be successful because I had no discipline or respect for authority in that instance became nothing more than white noise in the background. In place of their words, my grandmother's gentle voice shared wisdom, prayers, and a message that would change my life.

In an almost poetic voice, she said, "Persevere, no matter what."

Little did she know her voice would be all that stood in front of me and failure more times than I would count for many years to come. It became my life's motto, a mantra that would comfort me in the toughest tasks and during the darkest storms.

When Staff Sergeant Martinez opened the passenger door of his brand-new silver Acura, while silently motioning his head for me to get in, it finally hit me. My time in California, with all its painful memories and fleeting comforts, was over. I took a deep breath, hugged my mom one last time, and tried to hold back tears. I glanced at my family, my mother's home that was once a place of comfort and sometimes mayhem, along with the familiar streets, and knew there was no turning back. On the ride to the hotel where I would spend my last night in California, the weight of a thousand "what ifs" pressed down on me, leaving me sleep deprived and running on adrenaline. For hours, my mind raced. What if everyone that said I won't make it was right? What if that flicker of light inside of me that was guiding my weary steps toward change was all in my head? The thought of turning back and changing my mind was strong and scary. Turn back to what? What did I possibly have to turn back to? I had been homeless for about a month after I had to move out of my apartment. I had nowhere to go, no money and no job. Turning back wasn't an option I would entertain. I clung to my grandmother's words and finally fell asleep.

As soon as I started dreaming, the ear-piercing alarm clock woke me. As I eagerly awaited my recruiter's arrival in front of the giant hotel, the crisp early morning air sent chills through my body. I instantly regretted not heeding my mother's advice to bring a sweater. Staff Sergeant Martinez drove me to the Sacramento International Airport where I would experience my first ever plane ride. The flight to South Carolina was a mix of nerves and wonder. Pressing my face against the tiny window, I watched the world below fade away. Every mile in the air felt like a minor victory over the gravity of my past, lifting me closer to the future I'd dreamed of, but could barely imagine.

My naive optimism met its first challenge the moment I set foot on base. The humidity was unlike anything I'd ever felt, thick and sticky, and the drill sergeants wasted no time laying into us. I was just another recruit to them, my bright-eyed hopes swallowed up in the grit and grind of their tireless demands. My recruiter prepared me as much as he possibly could for what was to come.

Most of it I forgot or zoned out, except for one thing. "Don't forget basic training is a head game, meant to break you down and build you back up. They designed everything you encounter to strengthen you. Just don't give up and don't take it personally."

Drill Sergeant Mateo, a 6-foot 5-inch, bodybuilder looking, intimidating specimen of a man, had a voice that could shake the foundation of a building, and he seemed to get a special thrill out of barking orders at us in the early morning hours. I could still hear my grandmother's voice in my head, the way she used to say, "Persevere, no matter what." I clung to her words, letting them echo through my mind as I pushed myself through grueling drills and marches. Many days, I thought I could not go on. My body ached, my feet blistered, and sleep was a luxury I barely remembered. But giving up wasn't an option; I had fought too hard just to get here. I refused to let anyone, least of all myself, tell me I wasn't strong enough.

Life in the barracks was a world apart from anything I had known. The other recruits shared stories of their homes, their childhoods, and the people they missed. I told them my stories too. At least the parts I could bear to say aloud. In those shared stories, I found a camaraderie I hadn't known was possible. We were all there, in a sense, to start over, each of us motivated by something that would cause us to leave the life we knew behind. Some joined because of family tradition, some faced a choice between the Army or jail, and others joined because it seemed like a fun, well-paying option. I joined the Military because of all the doubts my family so eagerly pointed out in their attempt to dissuade me. My lack of respect for authority, lack of discipline and need for structure were the motivating factors that led me to join. My family was right: those were all areas in which I struggled, and I could recognize that the only way I was going to change and become someone in whom I could be proud was to put myself in an environment where I would have no choice but to learn those essential life skills.

As an adventurous outdoorsy kid growing up, I was no stranger to bugs, and frequently moving around from home to home, I encountered my fair share of creepy crawlies. They were practically roommates. Nothing in California prepared me for the creatures I would encounter on the East Coast. On one especially humid night, it was my turn to stand guard and monitor the barracks as my fellow soldiers desperately fueled up on rest. While performing the extensive list of nightly duties, I quietly mopped the floor, moving stealthily to not wake anyone. Out of the corner of my eye, I detected movement, too small to be a rodent but too big to be any kind of creature with which I was familiar. As I got closer, I saw what I could only describe as a giant cockroach on steroids, and it had wings. My curiosity led me closer, but my lack of knowledge about this new creature cautioned me not to get too close. As I tried to shoo it away with the mop, I thought, surely, I will scare it off and tell my fellow soldiers about this bionic creature I encountered during the night's watch. Pushing the mop toward the giant bug backfired instantly. Instead of fleeing to safety, this damn bug scurried up the mop head. I threw that mop and screamed loudly, waking up half the room. My erratic behavior and the commotion of my fellow soldiers caught the Drill Sergeant's attention that was patrolling the hallways. He rushed in, flipped on all the lights, and chewed me out, resulting in the entire room waking up.

In between his frustrated barks, he explained it was just a water bug.

"What the heck is a water bug? That was a giant cockroach with wings!" I cried out.

He asked where I was from and how I did not know what a water bug was.

"California," I replied, "And we don't have those there. California cockroaches are small, about the size of a pencil eraser, not the size of a chicken nugget."

His once agitated demeanor changed, and he ordered everyone to go back to sleep and for me to finish my duties.

Although the lights were off, I could feel the burning glares of pissed-off soldiers, their silent resentment cutting through the darkness. Because the soldiers' sleep was interrupted, and training was only a few hours away, I became Public Enemy Number One. Part of me felt guilty for my exaggerated response and the other part of me chuckled as I thought back on my encounter with the alien cockroach, otherwise known as a water bug.

After eight weeks of intense training, I made it. I graduated from basic training and now had the privilege of calling myself a soldier. My excitement quickly faded as my comrades shared the occupations they had each chosen and where they were heading for the next phase of their training. The excitement arose as they shared their jobs and linked up with fellow soldiers who had chosen the same job. Infantry, Intelligence, Medic, Transportation, they all sized each other up and compared jobs. I stood silently and slowly tried to remove myself from the inevitable inquiry about what job I chose. Just as I thought I might escape and avoid this line of questioning, I heard, "Private Brooks! What will your MOS be?" The Army's acronym for job descriptions. I froze, clinched my eyes and bit my lip. *Damn,* I thought, *Damn it, they caught me.*

I turned around and replied, "I don't have an MOS yet."

Suddenly, all eyes were on me and inquiring minds wanted to know how I could join without choosing a job. In my panic and inability to come up with a believable lie, I admitted to the group that because my scores on the ASVAB were so low I entered with the expectation that after basic training, depending on the needs of the Army, I would be offered three jobs and would have to choose one. They would offer three jobs that lacked personnel, jobs nobody wanted, but were necessary for the Army's operation.

I could see the pity in their eyes and my embarrassment sent a wave of heat rushing through my body, landing straight on my face. After turning red and taking in their stares of pity and judgment, I left without uttering a word. I felt so ashamed, despite just graduating basic training and enduring the toughest eight weeks of my life. The Drill Sergeant summoned me and three other soldiers later that day. He took us in a van; we'd all have to choose careers we never imagined because our scores weren't high enough. As I sat in a crowded office filled with soldiers of all different ranks, I passed the time by trying to identify each of their ranks and the proper names to go along with them.

Finally, I heard someone yell, "Private Brooks!" I eagerly stood and made my way to the window.

"Are you Private Brooks?"

"Yes Ma'am, I mean Yes Sergeant." Crap, I knew better than to call a Sergeant Ma'am.

The now irritated Sergeant handed me a paper with my three MOS offerings on it. Number one was a Laundry and Bath Specialist.

Looking up, confused, before I could ask, she said, "You will do people's laundry."

Desperate to read the next offering, I looked down, and it read Cook. I thought, *That can't be bad.* I had trained as a cook when I was working at IHOP and liked it. Looking at the last job offer, I saw it was for a Personnel Service Specialist. The Sergeant must have been through this song and dance many times before. She must have expected my confusion and many questions, because she snatched the paper out of my hand.

"Laundry and Bath Specialists do other Soldier's laundry; Cooks work in the dining facility and go to work while everyone is still asleep and have to go to the field whenever other units go for training, which is often; and Personnel Service Specialists sit at a desk and do paperwork," she barked.

I thought about each for a moment and recognized my dislike for doing my own laundry and remembered the hours we would spend at the laundromat as a child and hated it. I then thought, *I really don't enjoy getting up early and don't want to be in the field all the time.* So, to me, there was only one obvious choice: Personnel Service Specialist, it was.

There was a bittersweet irony attached to my new job. High school is when I first encountered computers, and I hated every minute. I didn't like change and learning how to use the computer and type on a keyboard was such a struggle for me. I barely passed my computer class with a D. Now I would choose a career working with the same thing I vowed to my teacher I would never do: Get a job where I had to use computers. Joke's on me; never say never.

Landing in Germany felt like stepping into a different life altogether. I was both exhilarated and terrified. It was like being nine years old again, walking into a new foster home, not knowing what awaited me on the other side. This time, the fear felt different. It wasn't paralyzing; it was energizing. As I walked through the airport, I saw people from places I had only read about, speaking languages I'd never heard. For a moment, I felt small, yet significant, as if I'd finally taken my place in a story much bigger than my own. With every step, I felt the past loosening its grip, even as it whispered to me, reminding me of everything I'd survived to get here. Walking through the bustling streets of Germany, hearing a language I barely understood, I knew I was starting over. For so long, I had equated success with escaping, with financial security, with anything that felt stable and permanent. Here I was, in a foreign country, with only my strength and resilience, and I realized my journey was about much more than just surviving. I was building something slowly, clumsily, but with a newfound sense of purpose. Germany became more than a duty station; it was a refuge. Each day, I felt the layers of my past peeling away, little by little, leaving room for something new to grow. The wounds didn't simply vanish. They were still there, under the surface, a part of me that would take time and care to heal.

Germany represented the beginning of a needed journey that would last a lifetime and involve so many opportunities for important lessons to be learned and opportunities to choose in which way I would learn those lessons. More often than not, I learned life's lessons the hard way, many of which strengthened me and some were results of unhealed trauma and false truths that took hold and shaped my belief system.

Leaving California and starting my Military career in Germany felt like walking away from the wreckage of a life I had barely survived, stepping onto that first plane not just as a passenger, but as a woman who refused to be defined by the pain she endured. Joining the military wasn't just a goodbye; it was a battle cry. A final break from a past that had tried to destroy me, and the first step toward a future I was finally ready to claim. It's no wonder I joined the military. I had been a soldier long before I ever put on a uniform. Even as a child, I lived with a heightened sense of vigilance, always watching my back, always looking over my shoulder, instinctively protecting myself and others in a world that had proven time and time again to be unsafe. Defending the weak, standing up for the vulnerable, it wasn't just a duty to which I would one day swear an oath. It was something that had been written into my very being from the start. Every hardship had sharpened me, every heartbreak had hardened me, and every betrayal had taught me resilience. The world had tried to bury me, but I had become the roots breaking through the concrete. This was my moment to step into a new chapter, a life beyond mere survival. My journey was far from over, but for the first time, I was walking into it with purpose, on my own terms, with my strength, and without fear.

EPILOGUE

THRIVING BEYOND SURVIVAL

LEAVING CALIFORNIA WAS MORE than a symbolic break from the past. It was a deliberate act of self-preservation. I wasn't just chasing a new beginning; I was putting physical and emotional distance between myself and the ghosts who still walked freely: Curtis, Derrick, and Anthony. Men who had caused unimaginable harm and yet moved through life untouched by consequence. California held too many shadows, too many chances for accidental run-ins, too many reminders. But in choosing to leave, I was also walking away from people I loved, fractured relationships with both my mother and father, and the siblings I shared through each of them.

I knew I was creating space between myself and my mother's children, Michael and Angela, and my father's children, Lewis, Dominique, and Alexander. The separation was painful, but necessary.

In time, something beautiful emerged from the pain. Lewis and I, once strangers linked only by blood, became best friends. We got stationed in the same city, which gave us the rare gift of proximity. That closeness allowed us to truly see each other. Lewis and his incredible wife, Stephanie, became pillars in my life, my safe harbor when storms rolled in. During some of my hardest years as a young single mother of three boys, they showed up for me without hesitation. They offered guidance, love, and stability. And to this day, they remain some of my most treasured allies.

My bond with Alexander and Dominique has deepened over the years too, slowly but meaningfully. As we've grown, we've carved out space for one another, healing through shared time and laughter, creating a connection that once seemed unreachable.

But not all relationships followed the same path. My connection with Michael and Angela, my mother's children, has never fully recovered. Curtis's abuse cast a long shadow, one that shaped how they saw me, or didn't. Time and distance widened the gap, but it was the silence, the unspoken truth they may never fully understand, that created a divide no phone call or social media message could mend. I carry a quiet grief for the relationship we could have had, if only the truth hadn't come with such unbearable weight.

Still, I move forward with a heart open to possibility, knowing some bonds mend slowly, and others may never heal. But I've learned that choosing myself doesn't mean abandoning love, it just means protecting the parts of me that are finally learning to thrive.

Time, patience, and the courage to engage in countless painful, uncomfortable, and vulnerable conversations have slowly mended what once felt permanently broken. My relationships with both my mother and father have evolved in ways I never thought possible. For years, I carried the weight of anger, confusion, and disappointment, unsure if true reconciliation could ever exist between us. But healing doesn't happen in silence, it happens in truth. And through that truth, something remarkable unfolded.

With my mother, there were moments filled with raw emotion, tears, long pauses, and trembling words, but there was also a willingness to listen, to hold space, and to sit with the pain rather than run from it. Slowly, the layers of misunderstanding and unspoken sorrow lifted, revealing a shared desire to reconnect and move forward, not by pretending the past never happened, but by honoring how far we've come.

My relationship with my father took its own shape. It wasn't immediate or easy, but it was intentional. Through open dialogue and a shared willingness to show up, messy, human, and imperfect, we repaired what once seemed irreparable. His presence in my life today isn't just symbolic; it's meaningful. He is here, engaged, and walking beside me in my healing process.

Together, they have become active participants in my journey, not just figures from my past, but pillars in my present. And in doing so, they've reminded me that love, when nurtured with truth and grace, can be resilient enough to survive even the deepest wounds.

My enlistment in the Army was not driven by any grand patriotic ambition. I wasn't dreaming of medals or rank. I was a young woman with no coherent plan, only a fierce determination to escape the life I had known, a life that pain, struggle, and survival had dictated. The military gave me something I had never honestly had before: stability, structure, and a purpose. It taught me discipline and showed me that my body and mind were far more substantial than I had ever believed. Basic training was grueling, but nothing compared to what I had already endured in life. I pushed through, proving to myself over and over again that I was not just a survivor, I was a fighter. The Army forced me to stand tall, to find my voice, and to believe in my strength, and that strength would be tested many times over the years to come.

Nothing in life, not even the military, could have prepared me for the most defining role I would ever take on: becoming a mother. Having three incredible boys and gaining two fantastic stepdaughters was my greatest joy and most significant challenge. I poured every ounce of love I had into those children, determined to break the cycle of trauma and pain that had haunted my childhood. Being a mother while still healing from my past was difficult. I made many mistakes, learned lessons the hard way, and wrestled with the shadows of my past while trying to build a brighter future for them. Motherhood was a battlefield of its own, balancing work, parenting, and the weight of my healing. Yet through it all, my children gave me purpose. They reminded me of what unconditional love looked like. They became my reason to keep pushing forward, even on the days when I didn't think I could.

For so long, I had mistaken pain for passion, and chaos for connection. I had convinced myself that love hurt, that relationships were something to survive rather than somewhere to flourish. I believed love was a war zone, a battlefield where one person always walked away wounded. Until I met Thaddeus.

He was unlike any man I had known. There was no need to decode his words, no reason to tiptoe around his moods, no fear of when the next storm would come. Thaddeus was patient in a way I had never experienced, not just with me, but with life itself. His kindness was genuine, not performed for attention, and he never raised his voice to prove a point, never asserted dominance to feel powerful. His presence alone was enough. Most importantly, he didn't try to fix me. He didn't see me as broken or fragile, nor did he demand I bury my past to make him more comfortable. Instead, he stood beside me, steady and unwavering, loving me through every phase of healing, every moment of growth, every scar left behind by the past. With him, I learned that love wasn't supposed to be a battlefield, a punishment, or a debt to be repaid. Love, in its purest form, was safe, steady, and freeing. And for the first time in my life, I didn't just believe in it, I finally felt worthy of it.

With Thaddeus came two beautiful stepdaughters and a rather annoyingly rambunctious dog. Together, we created a family bound by love and intention. Blending our family hasn't been easy, but it was always worth it. Now, fourteen years later, I wake up every morning grateful for the love we've built. I am thankful for a marriage that feels like home. I am grateful for a man who reminds me daily that love is not about possession but partnership.

Healing is not a finish line. It is a lifelong process, and one I am still walking. Therapy has become a constant in my life, a space where I continue to unravel the past while building my future. Some days are more complex than others. Some days, the old wounds resurface, trying to convince me I am still the broken little girl who never felt safe. However, I'm wiser now. I practice showing myself grace and compassion and allow myself to feel, grow, and evolve. Forgiveness, I've learned, is not about excusing those who hurt me, but freeing myself from resentment. I have stopped carrying burdens that were never mine to hold.

For too long, I believed survival was enough. Survival is not the end goal. Thriving is. Now, I live. I love, I thrive, and I have broken generational cycles, choosing to raise my children in a home filled with love, security, and healing. A life I once thought impossible, I have now built. A life where I am not just the product of my past, but the author of my future. Every struggle, heartbreak, and moment I thought I would never make it through led me here. And I am still here. I am still growing, still learning, and still thriving.

Christina Duke

Resources

A Personal Note

If you're reading this, know that you are not alone. Whether you're at the beginning of your healing journey or somewhere in the messy middle, there are people and tools ready to walk beside you. Healing is not about being perfect, it's about being present, being seen, and giving yourself the compassion you always deserved.

Please use these resources as a starting point. The courage it takes to ask for help is a sign of strength, not weakness.

With love and solidarity,
—Christina Duke

Resources for Healing and Support

Healing from trauma, especially childhood sexual abuse, is not a linear path. This journey often requires a combination of tools, support systems, and professional care. Below is a list of trusted resources that may help guide you or a loved one toward recovery, understanding, and empowerment.

Crisis & Emergency Support

National Sexual Assault Hotline (RAINN)
1-800-656-HOPE (4673)
www.rainn.org
24/7 confidential support for survivors of sexual violence.

Suicide & Crisis Lifeline (U.S.)
Call or Text 988
Immediate support for mental health crises, suicidal thoughts, or emotional distress.

The Trevor Project (LGBTQ+ Youth Support)
1-866-488-7386 | Text "START" to 678678
www.thetrevorproject.org

Therapy & Trauma Recovery

Psychology Today Therapist Finder
www.psychologytoday.com
Find licensed therapists in your area, including those specializing in trauma, childhood abuse, and PTSD.

Therapy for Black Girls
www.therapyforblackgirls.com
Culturally competent mental health support and directories.

Open Path Collective
www.openpathcollective.org
Affordable therapy options for individuals and families without insurance.

Sidran Institute
www.sidran.org
Education and resources for people dealing with traumatic stress and dissociation.

Mindfulness & Self-Regulation Tools

Insight Timer (App)–Free meditations, trauma-sensitive breath work & grounding practices

Calm App–Mindfulness, sleep support, and emotional regulation exercises

Yoga With Adriene (YouTube)–Free, gentle yoga practices, including emotional release and grounding

Support Groups & Communities

Adult Survivors of Child Abuse (ASCA)

www.ascasupport.org

Free support groups (in-person & online) for adult survivors of childhood abuse.

Survivors Network of Those Abused by Priests (SNAP)

www.snapnetwork.org

Military & Veteran Support (if applicable)

Veterans Crisis Line–Dial 988 then press 1

www.veteranscrisisline.net

Give an Hour–Free mental health care for military and veterans

www.giveanhour.org

Books That Inspire Healing

Memoirs That Illuminate Mental Health & Survival

1. *The Body Keeps the Score* by Dr. Bessel van der Kolk
   A foundational book on how trauma reshapes the body and brain, and how healing is possible through mind-body therapies.
2. *What My Bones Know* by Stephanie Foo
   A powerful memoir of living with complex PTSD, identity, and reclaiming wholeness as a woman of color.
3. *Maybe You Should Talk to Someone by Lori Gottlieb*

A therapist's hilarious and heartbreaking account of her own therapy journey, reminding us that healing is universal.

4. *I'm Glad My Mom Died* by Jennette McCurdy
   A brutally honest look at fame, abuse, and recovery that is both darkly humorous and emotionally honest.

5. *The Collected Schizophrenias* by Esmé Weijun Wang
   A deeply personal and intellectual exploration of living with chronic mental illness.

Guided Healing & Therapeutic Tools

6. *Complex PTSD: From Surviving to Thriving* by Pete Walker
   A must-read for survivors of childhood trauma looking for deep, practical healing tools.

7. *It Didn't Start with You* by Mark Wolynn
   Unpacking inherited family trauma and how to stop cycles passed down through generations.

8. *Healing the Child Within* by Charles L. Whitfield
   Focuses on re-parenting the wounded inner child and building a healthy self.

9. *Radical Acceptance* by Tara Brach
   A compassionate guide on how mindfulness and self-compassion can break cycles of shame and self-doubt.

10. *The Gifts of Imperfection* by Brené Brown
    Encourages readers to embrace vulnerability and imperfection as sources of strength and authenticity.

Mindfulness, Emotional Balance & Spiritual Healing

11. *The Book of Awakening* by Mark Nepo
    Daily reflections and meditations to support emotional clarity and gratitude during hard seasons.

12. *Untamed* by Glennon Doyle

A fierce and raw call to live your truth and shed the conditioning of people-pleasing.

13. *Self-Compassion: The Proven Power of Being Kind to Yourself* by Dr. Kristin Neff

Explores how self-kindness radically shifts healing and resilience.

14. *How to Do the Work* by Dr. Nicole LePera (The Holistic Psychologist)

Blends psychology, neuroscience, and spiritual growth into a roadmap for self-healing.

15. *Man's Search for Meaning* by Viktor E. Frankl

A Holocaust survivor's timeless lesson that purpose can be found even in the darkest circumstances.